MYSTERY
MAZES ADULTS

MAZE DETECTIVE

ActivityCrusades

Published by Speedy Publishing Canada Limited

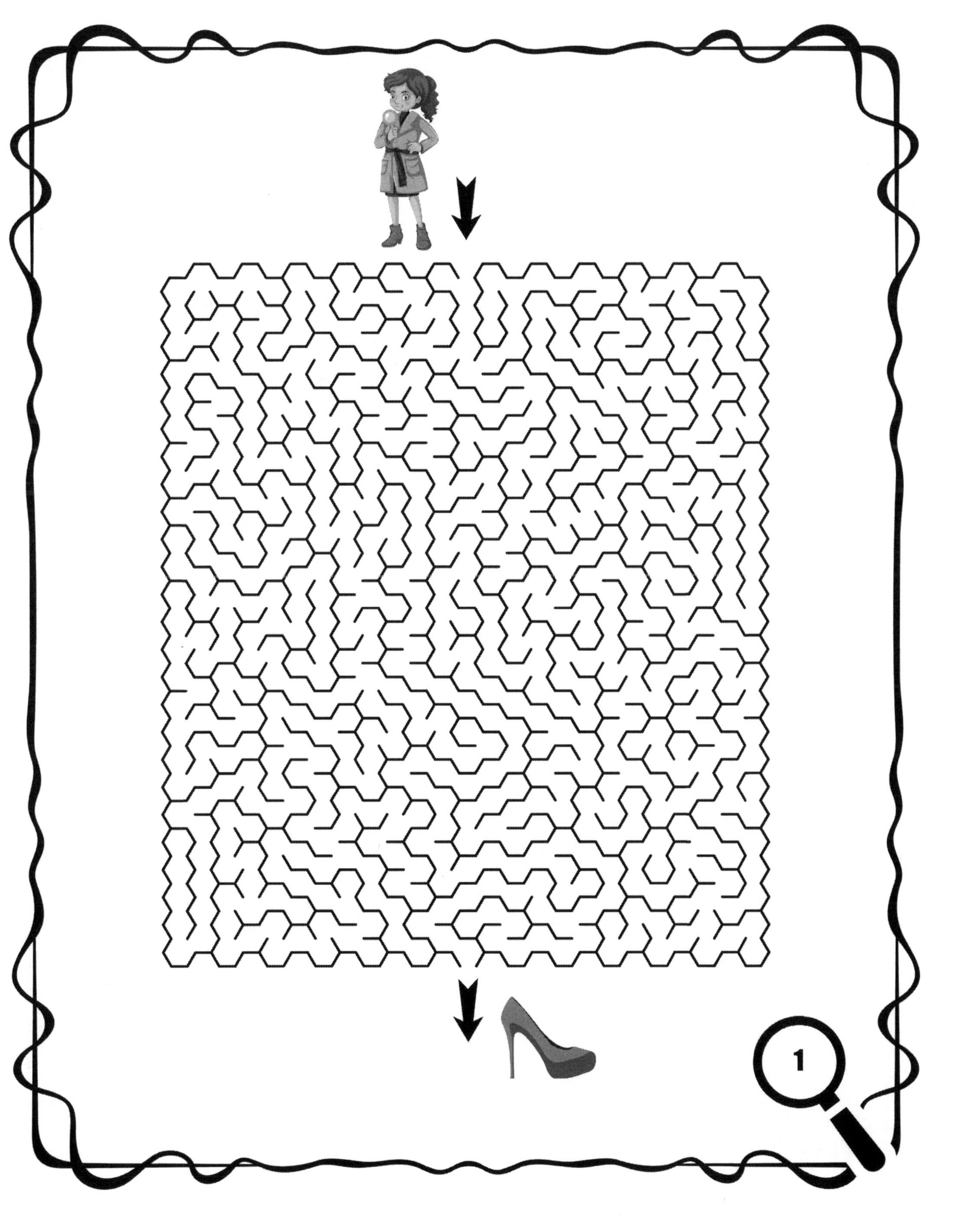

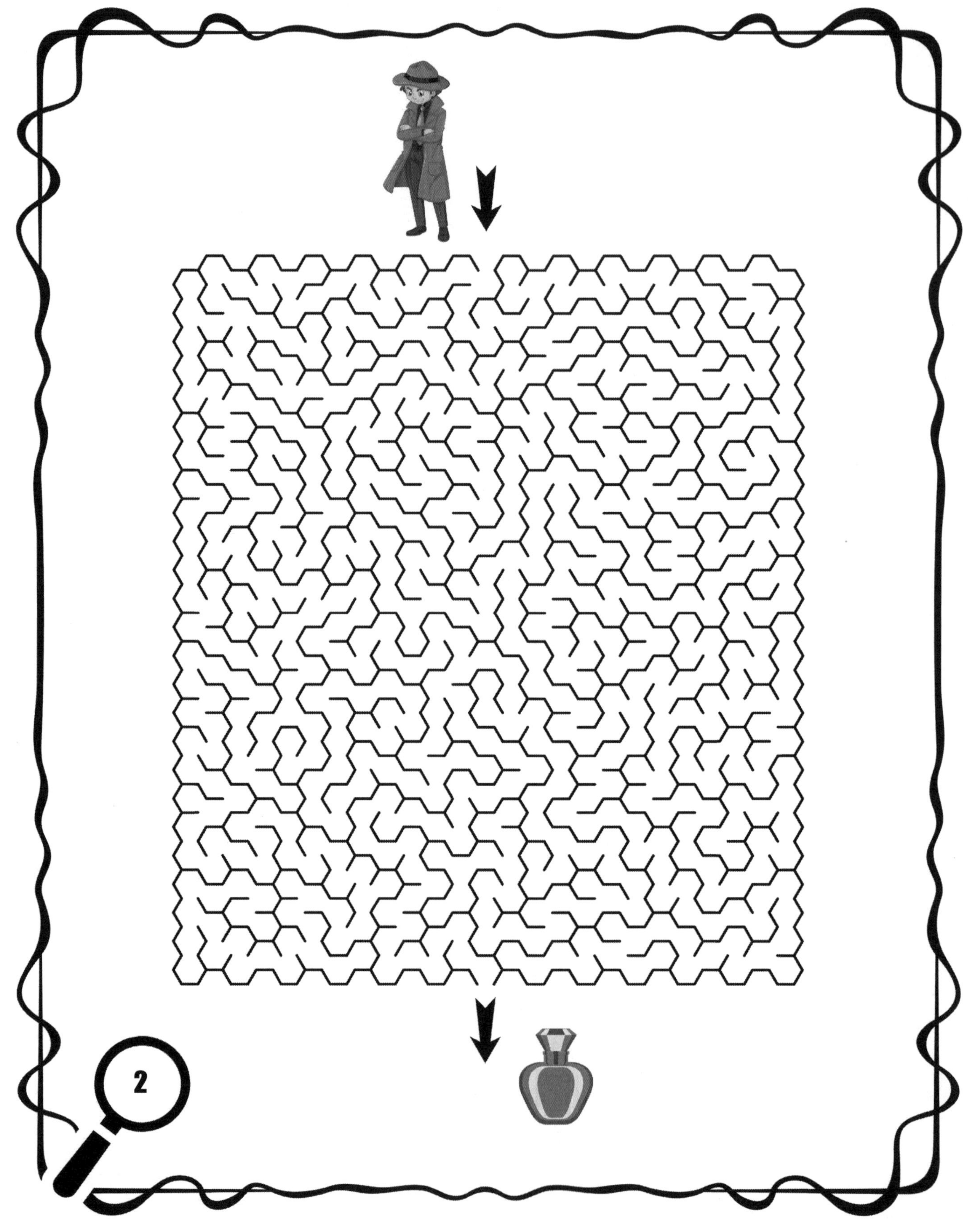
2

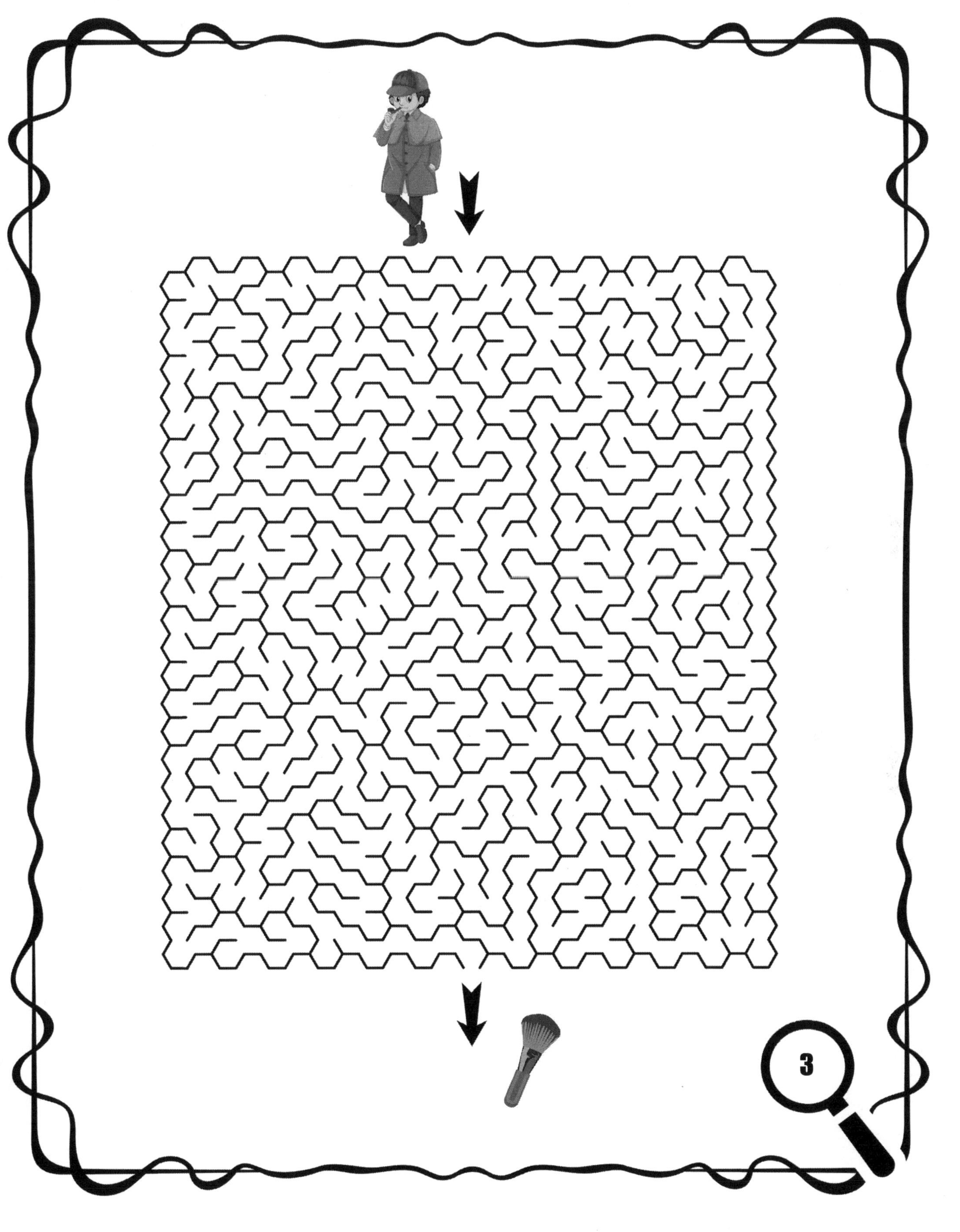
3

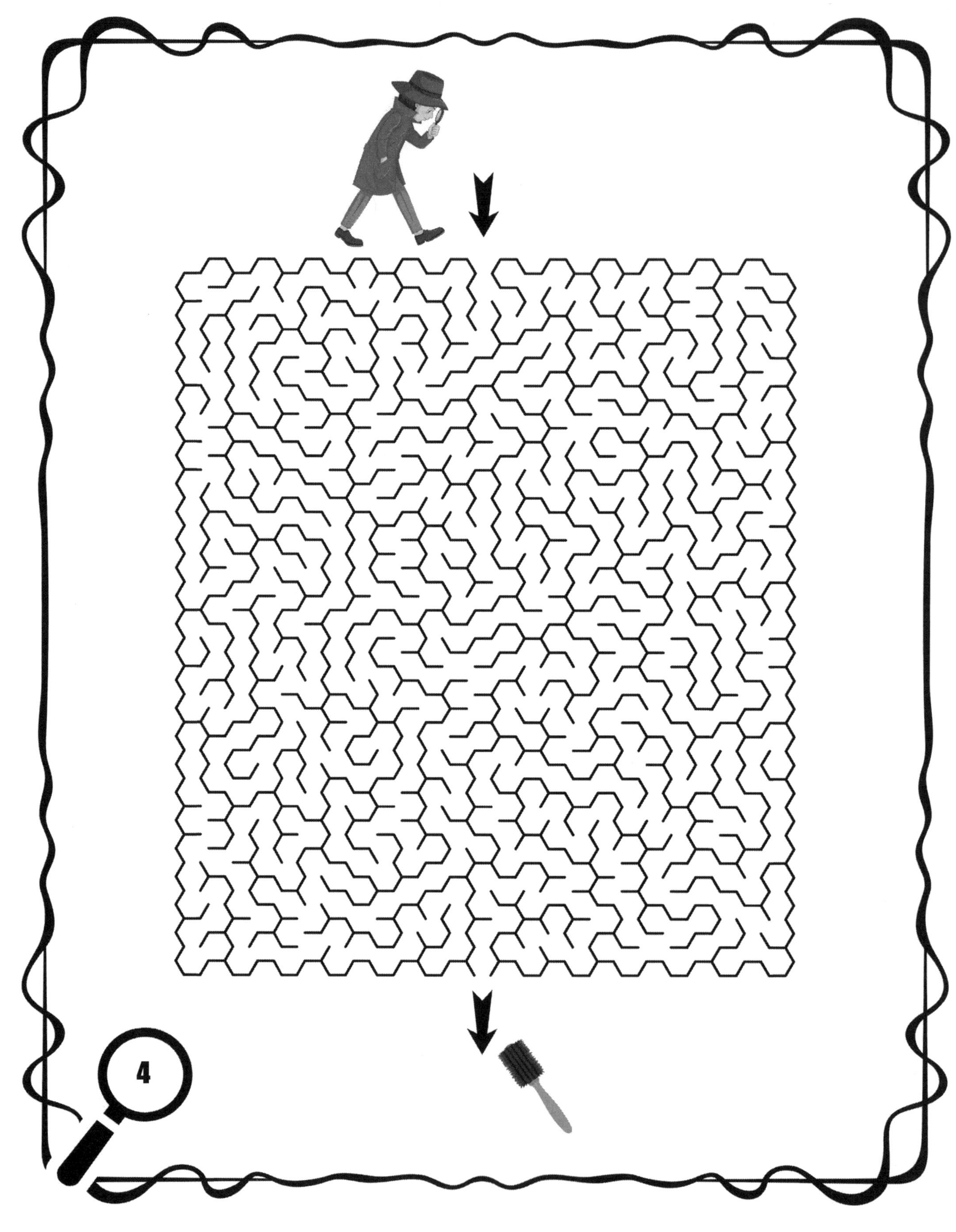

4

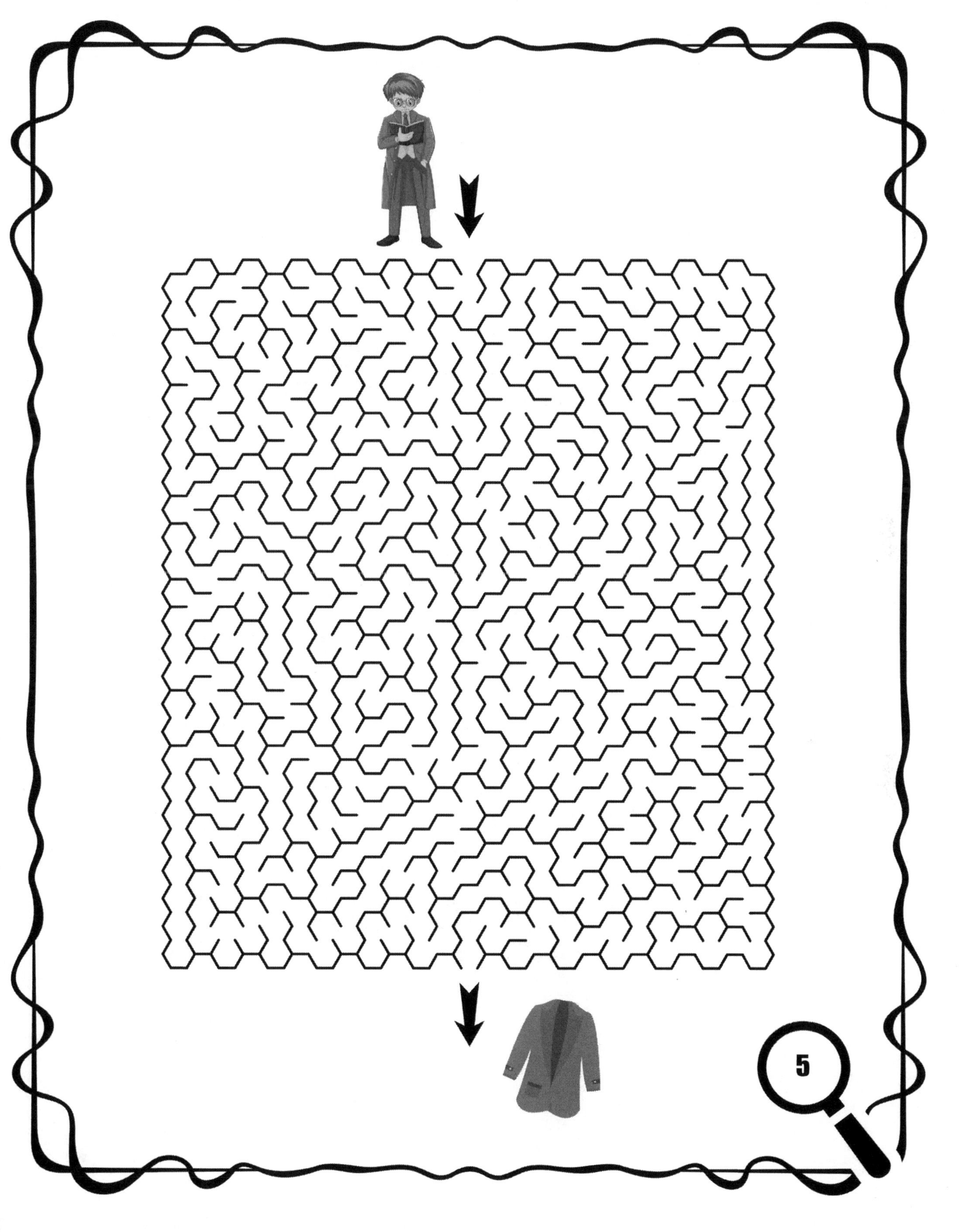

5

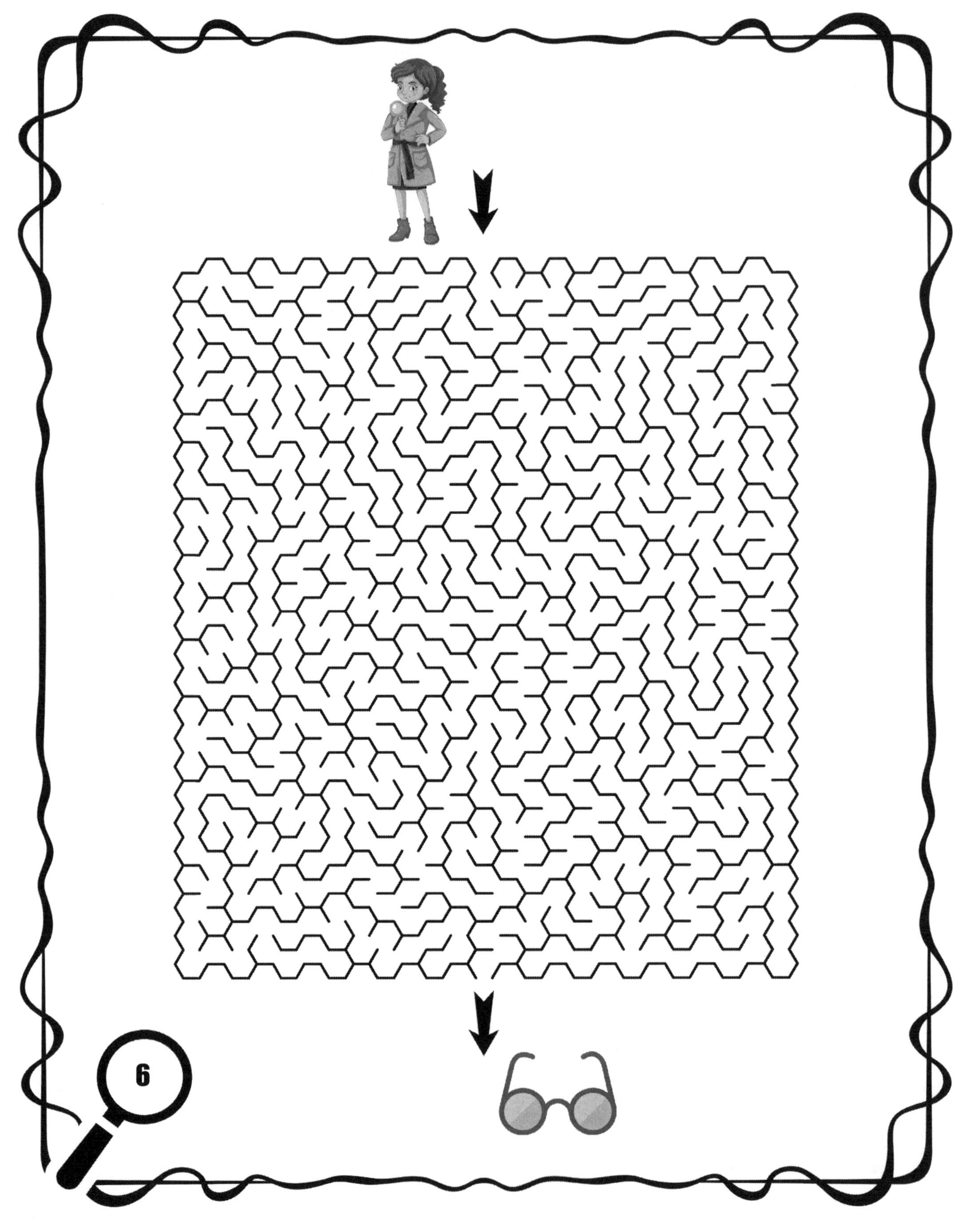

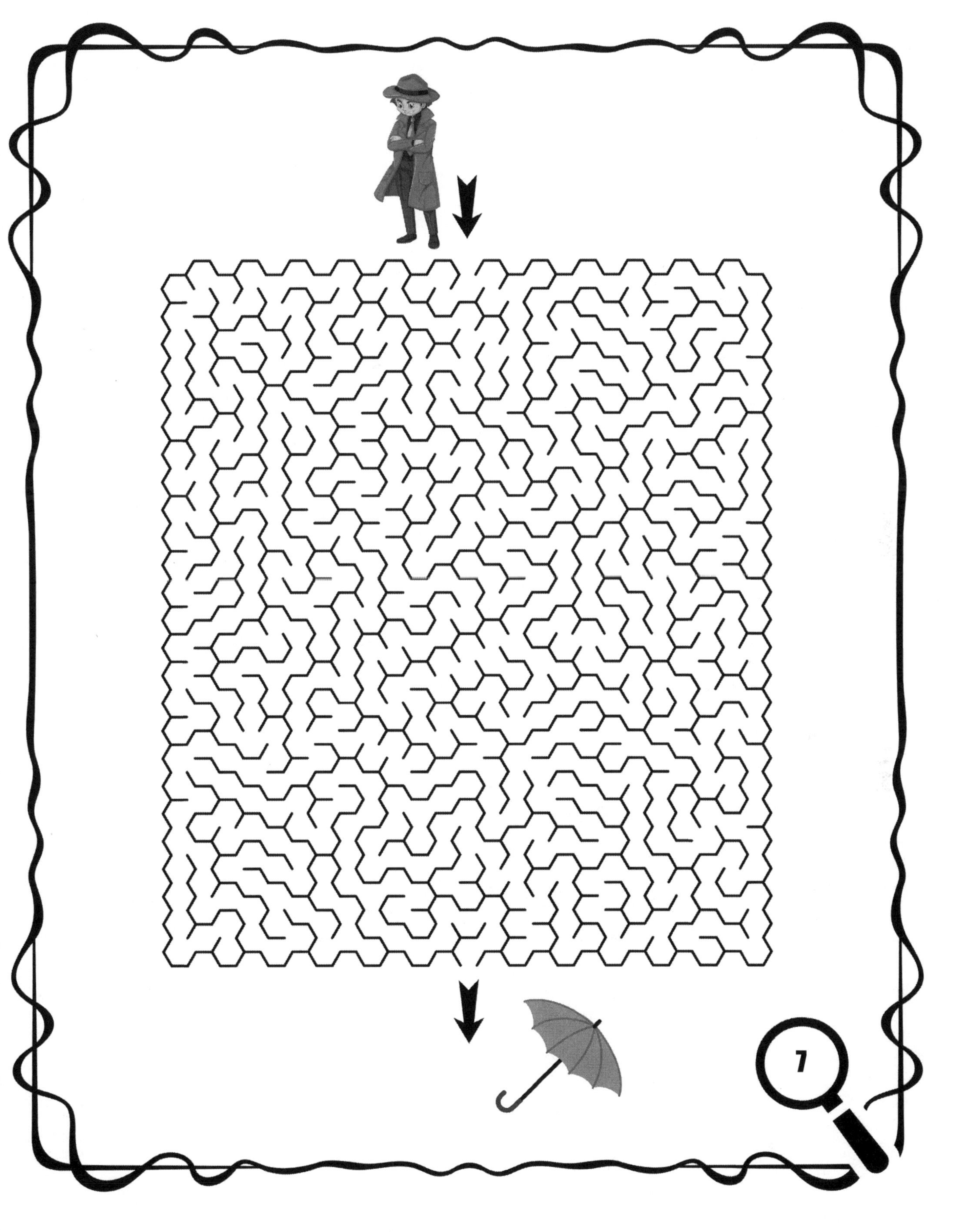

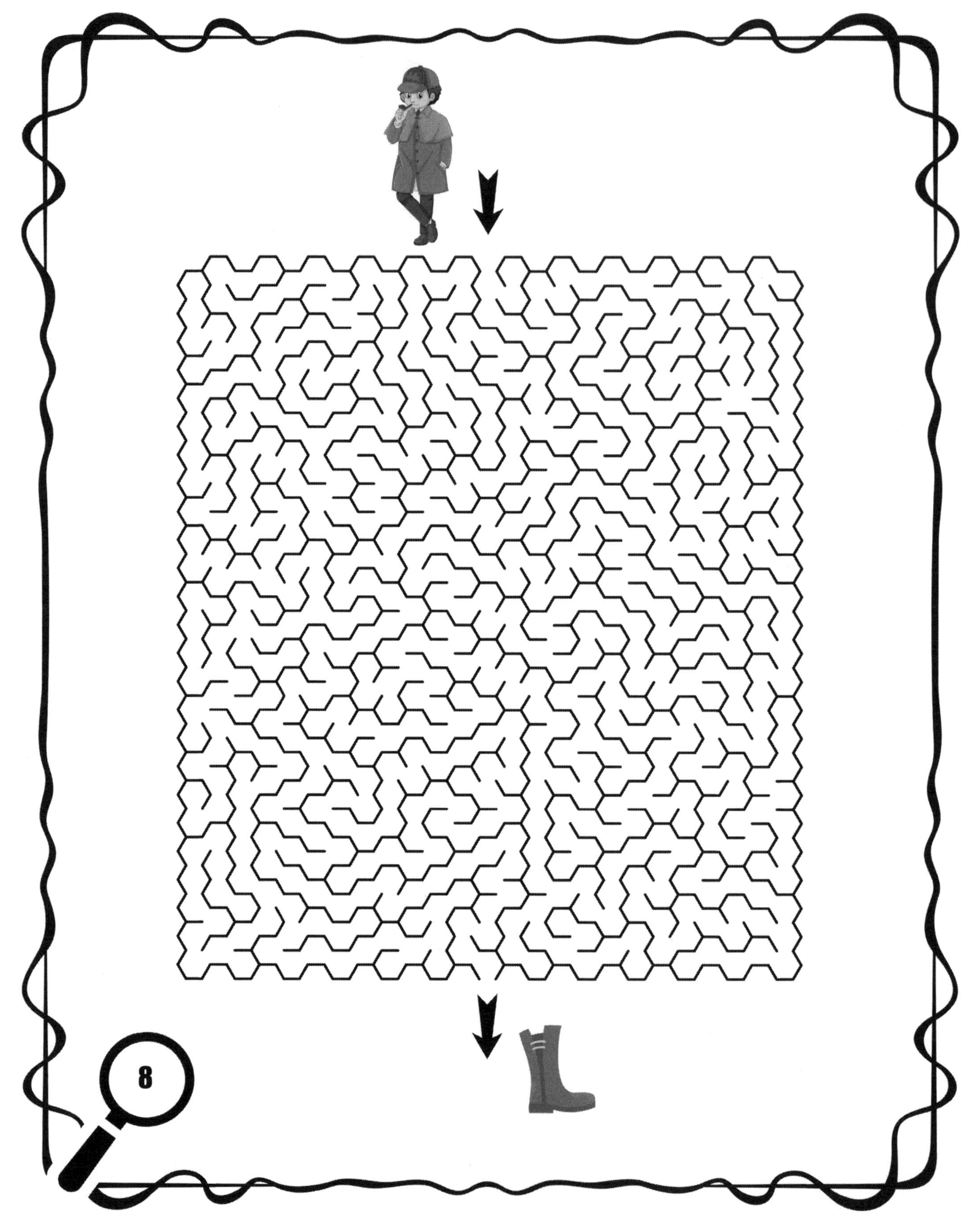

9

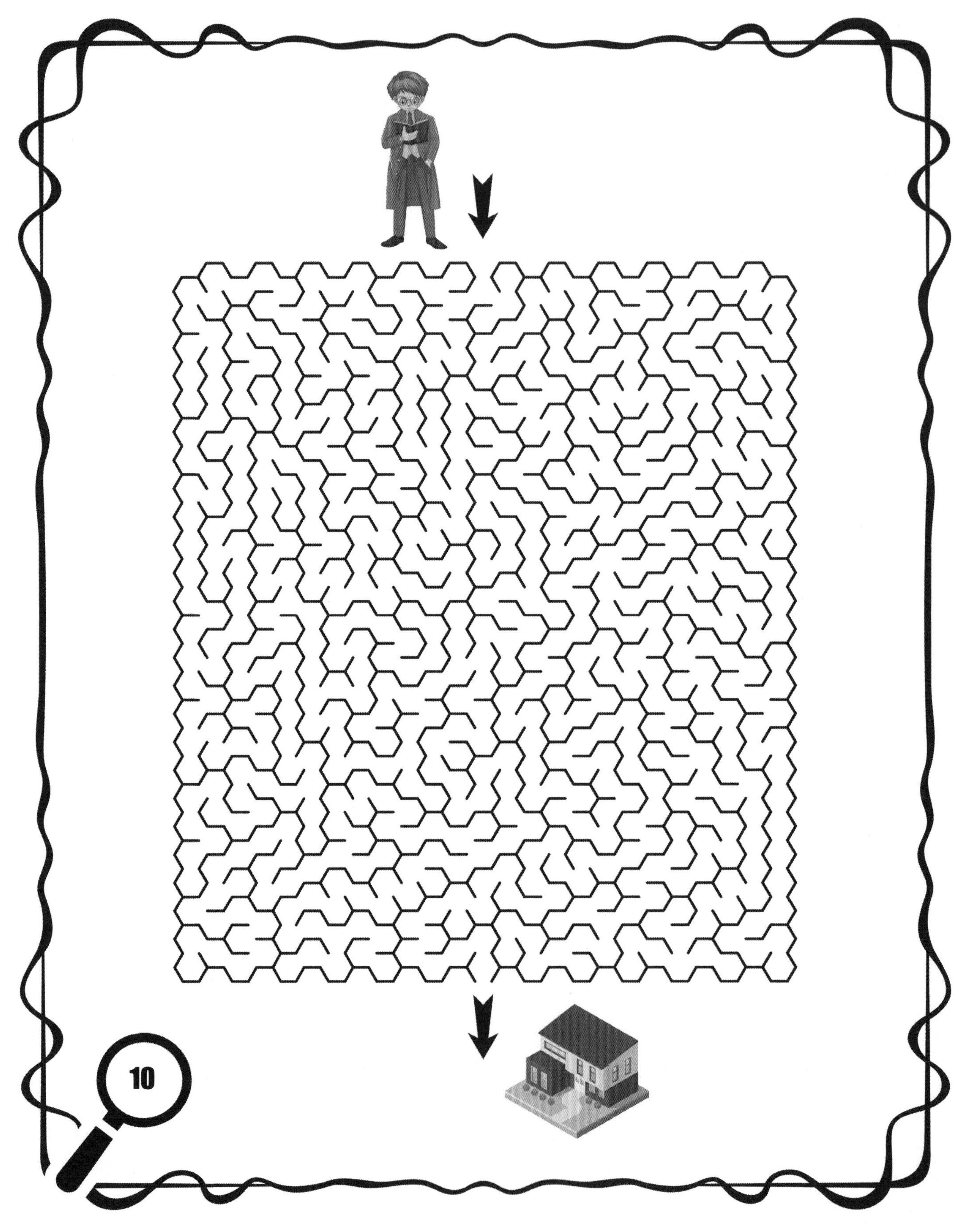

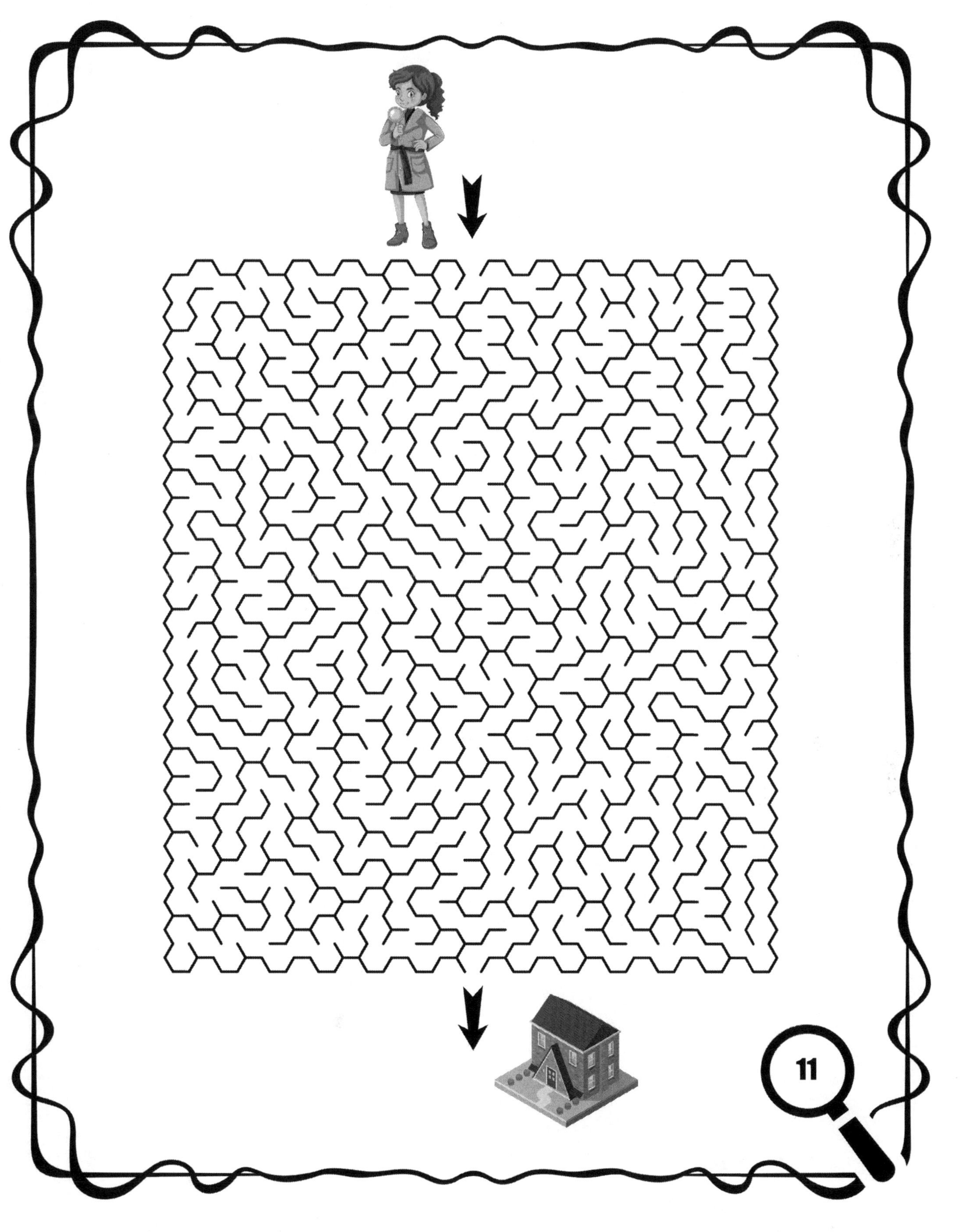

11

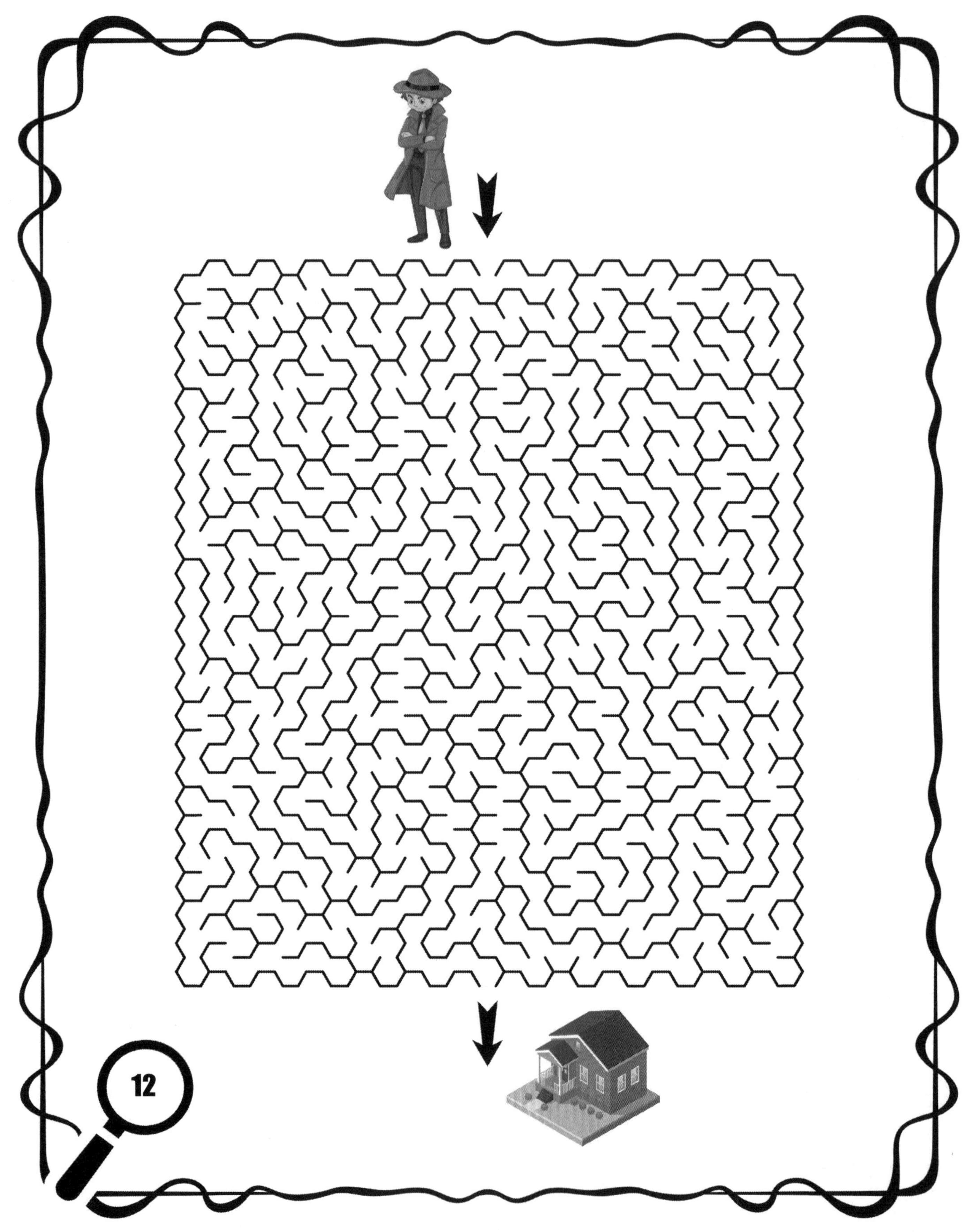

12

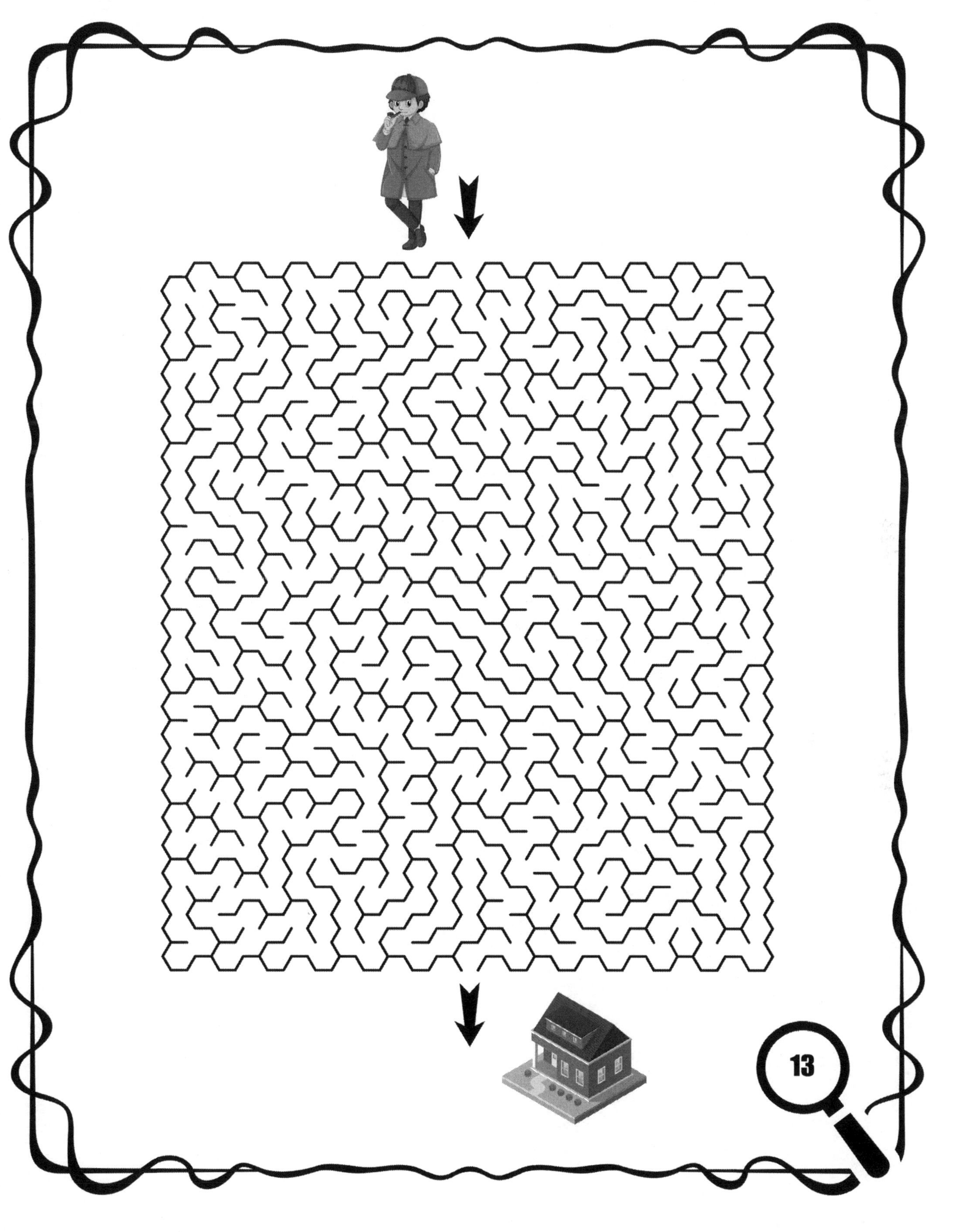

13

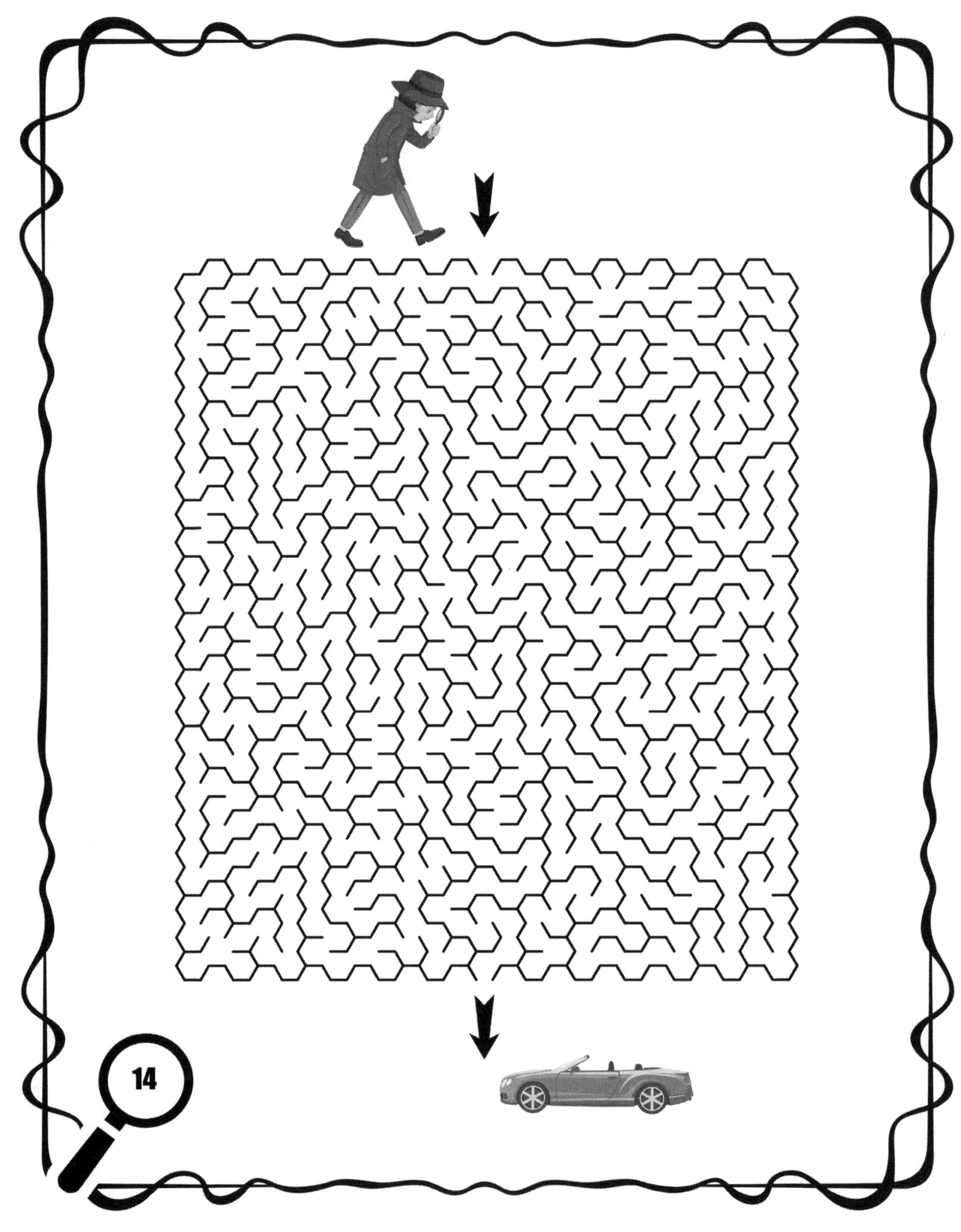

14

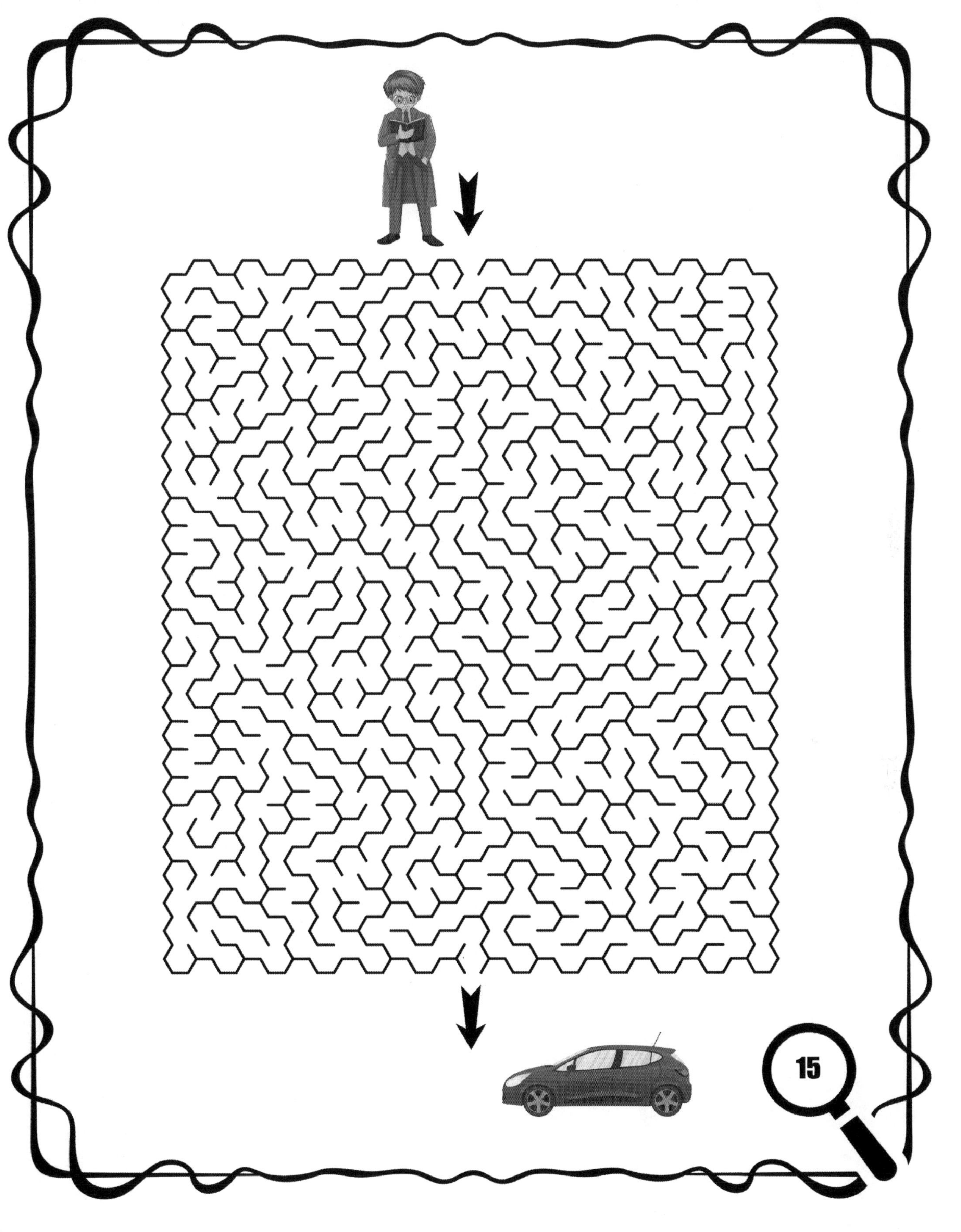

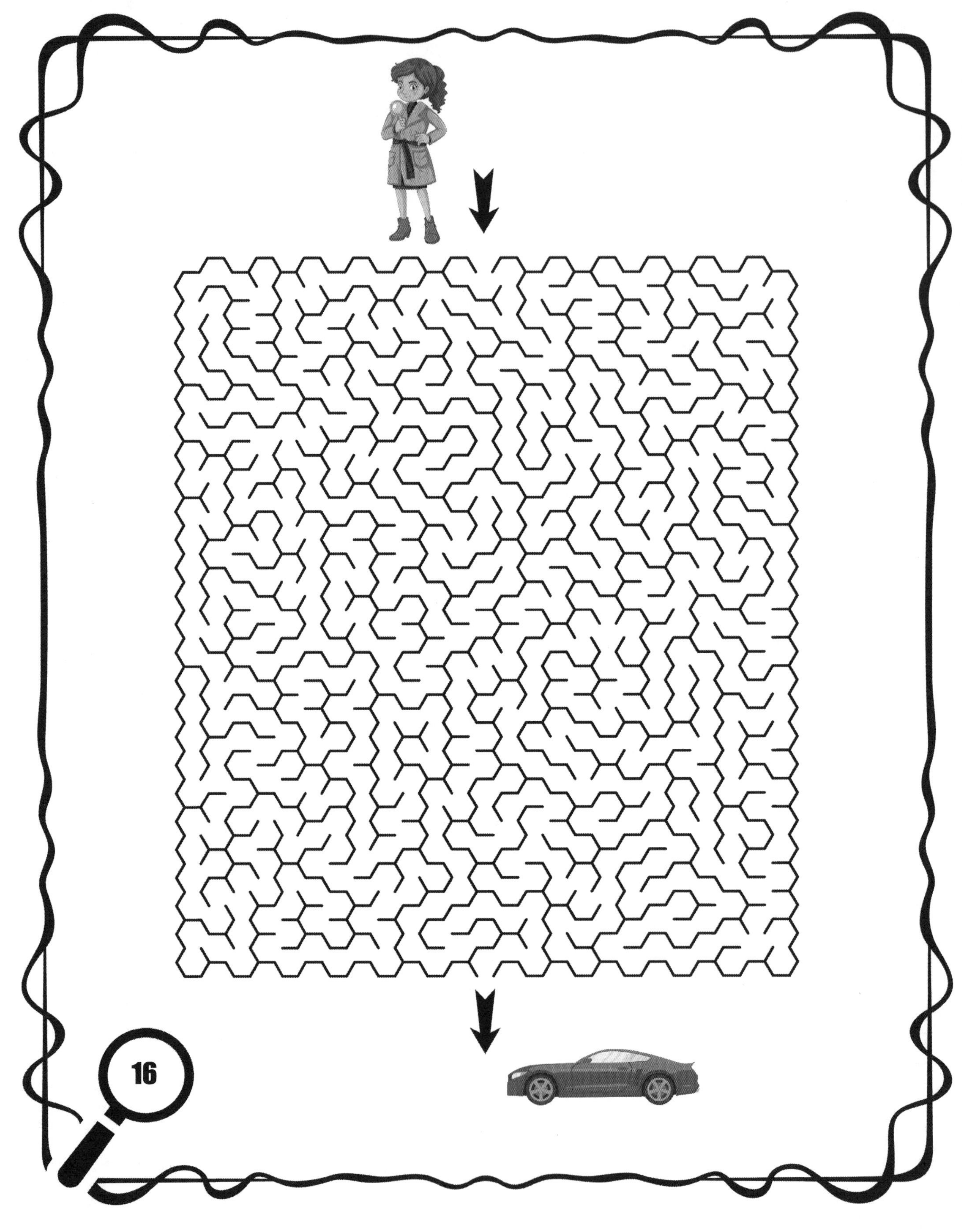

16

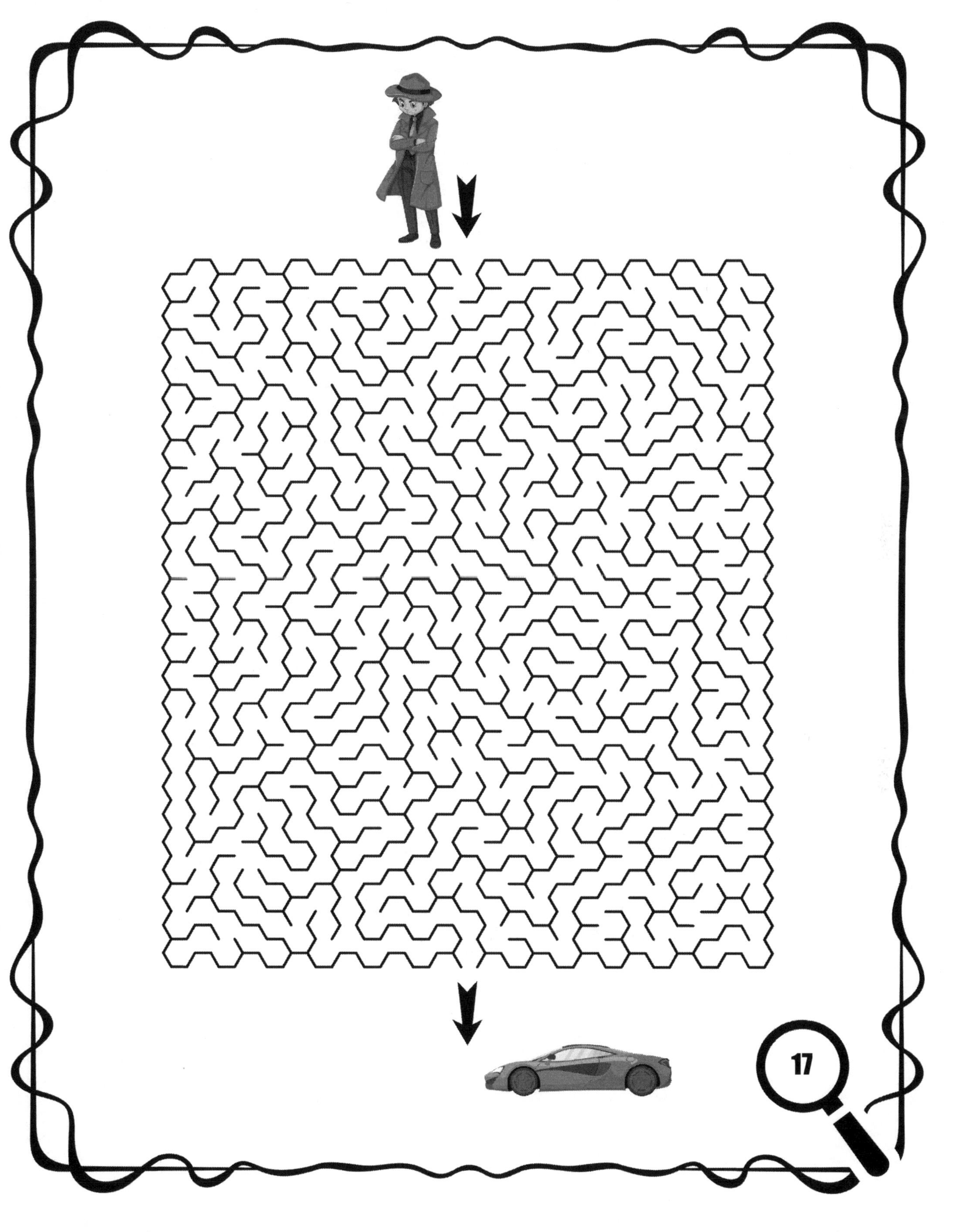

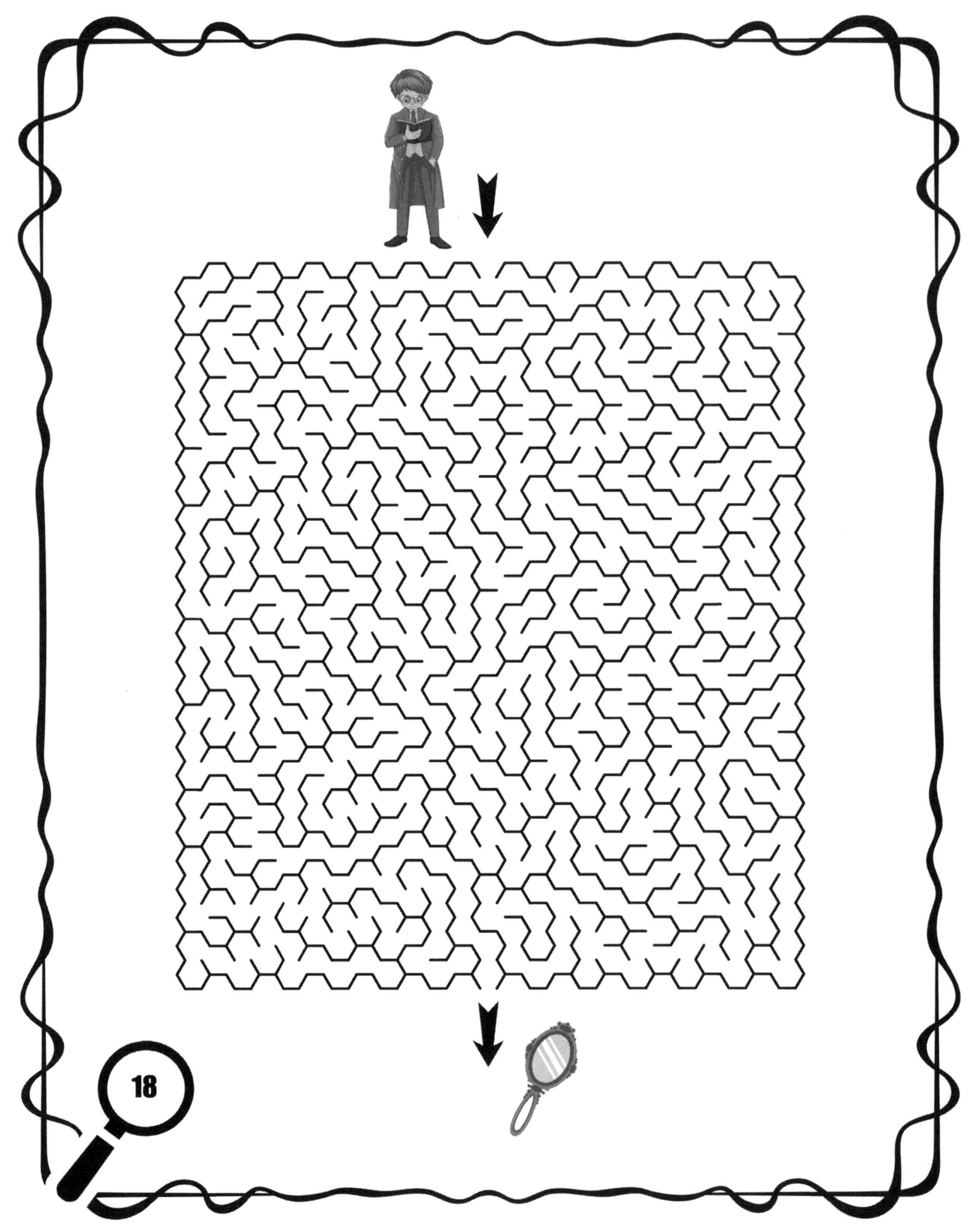

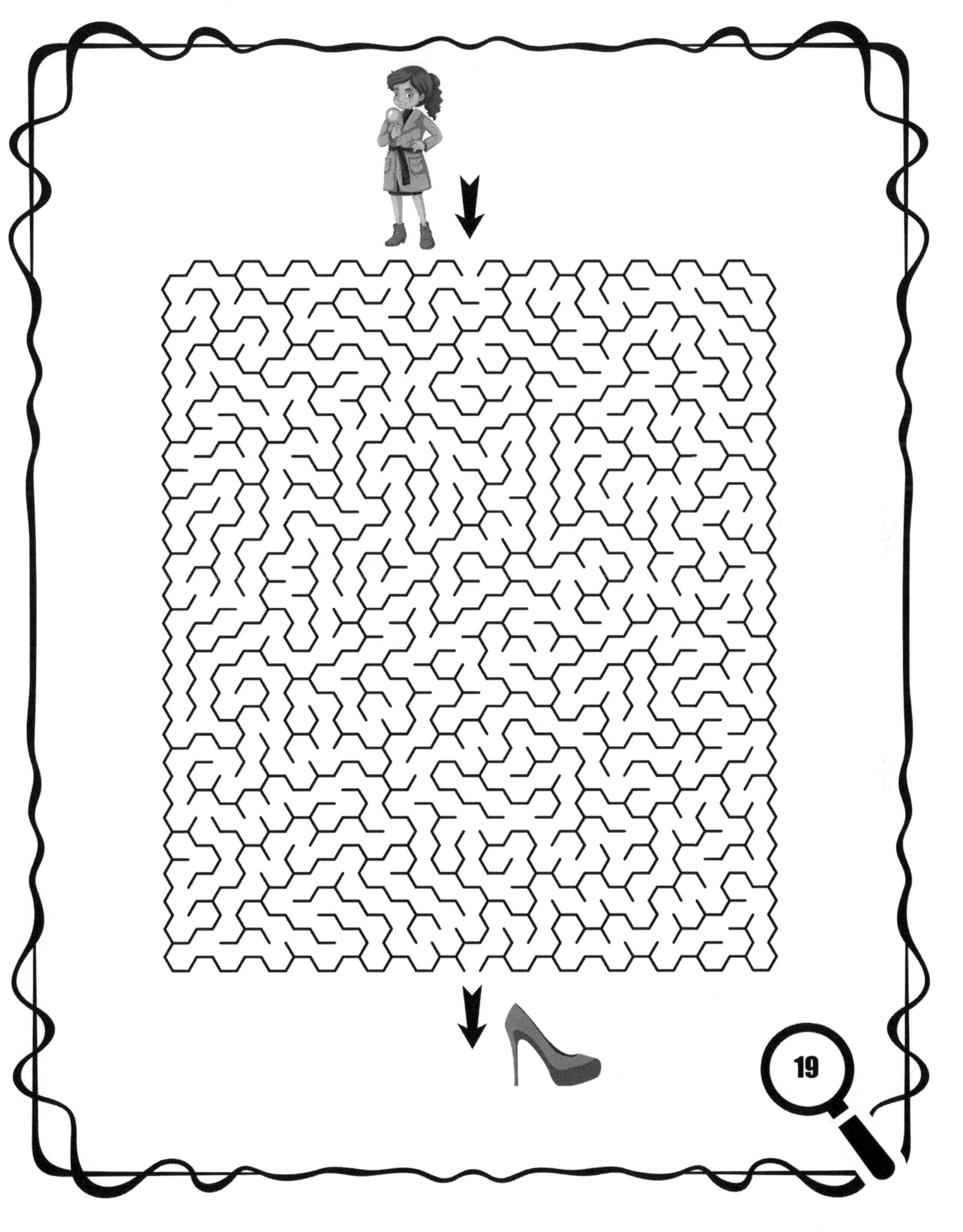

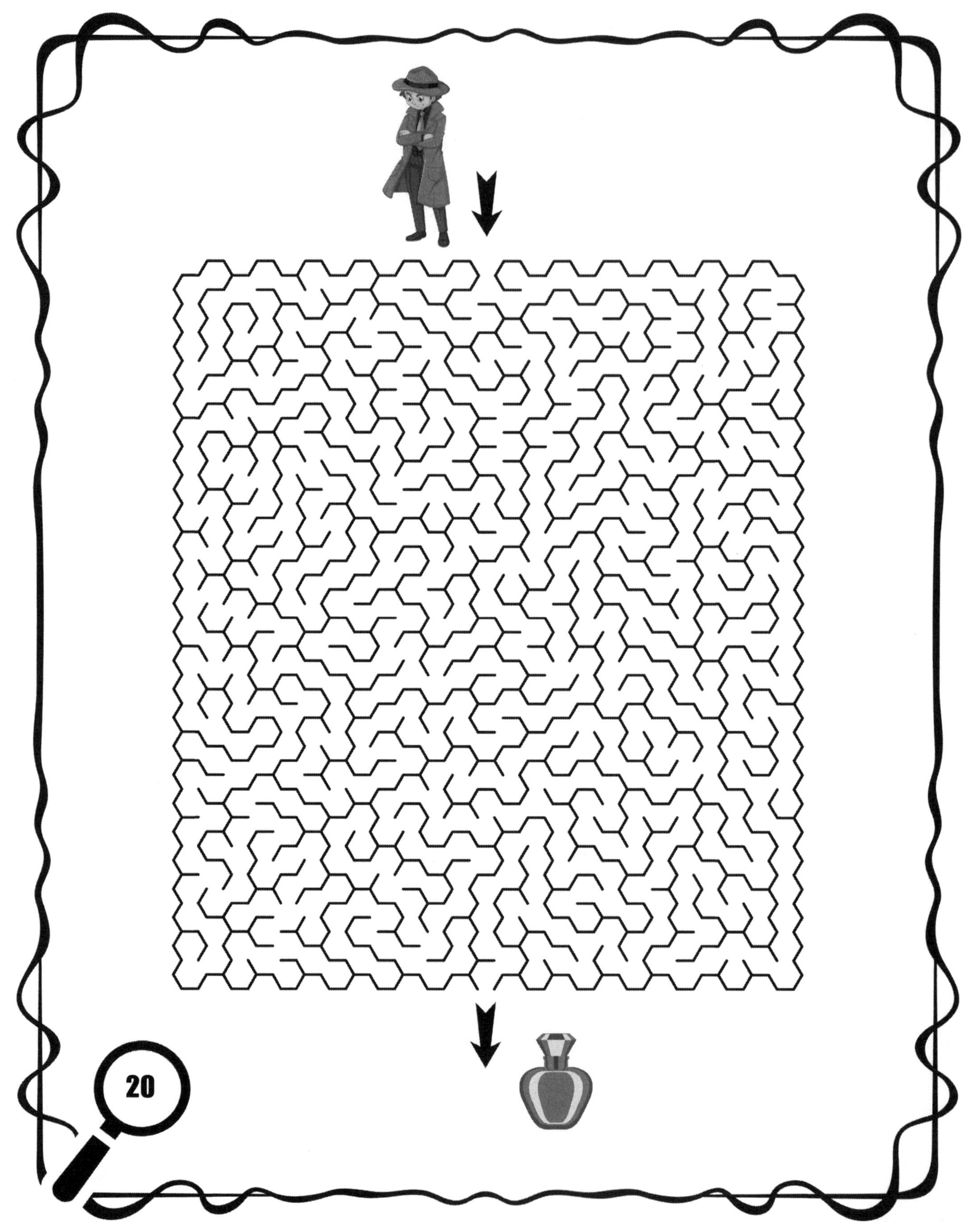

20

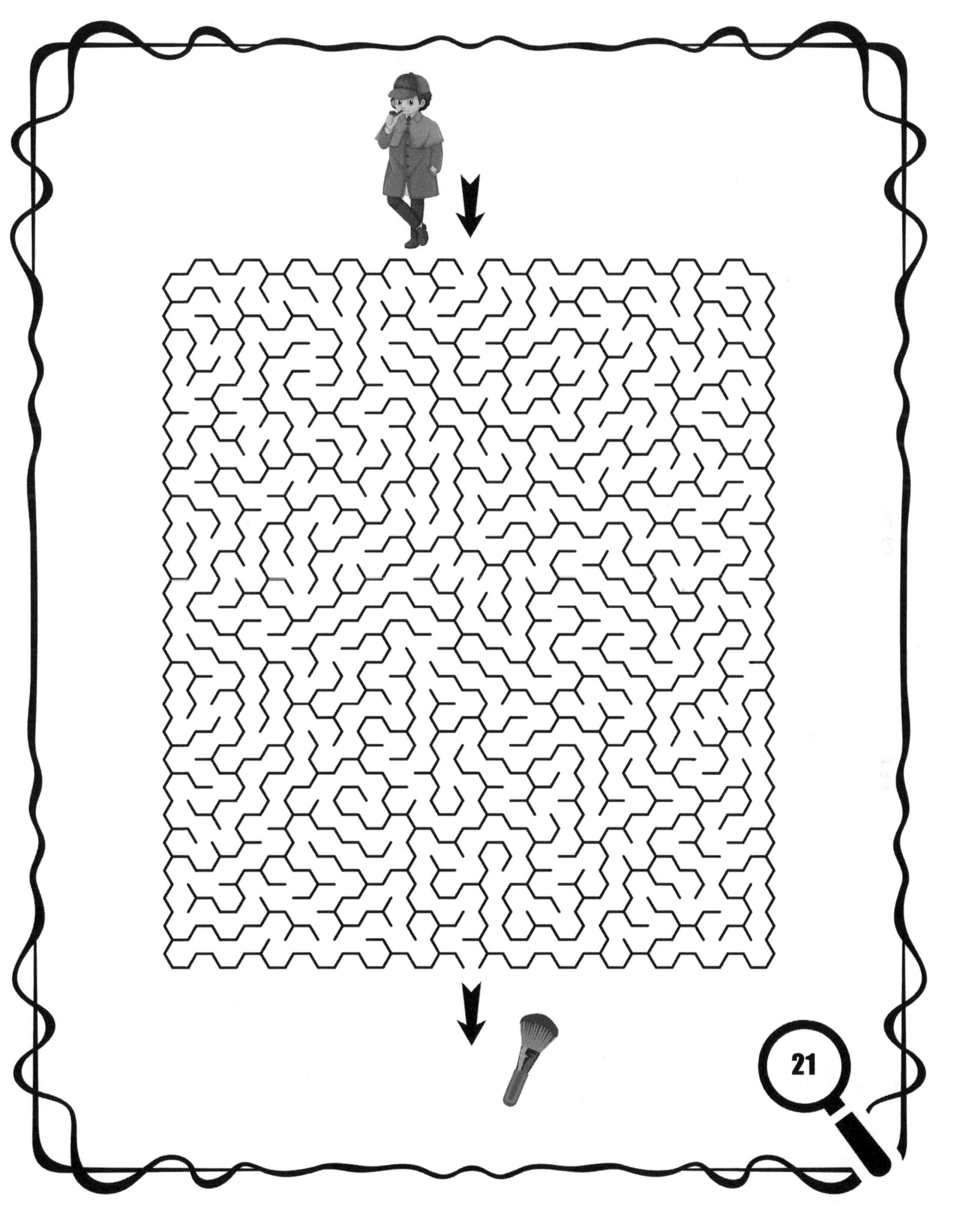
21

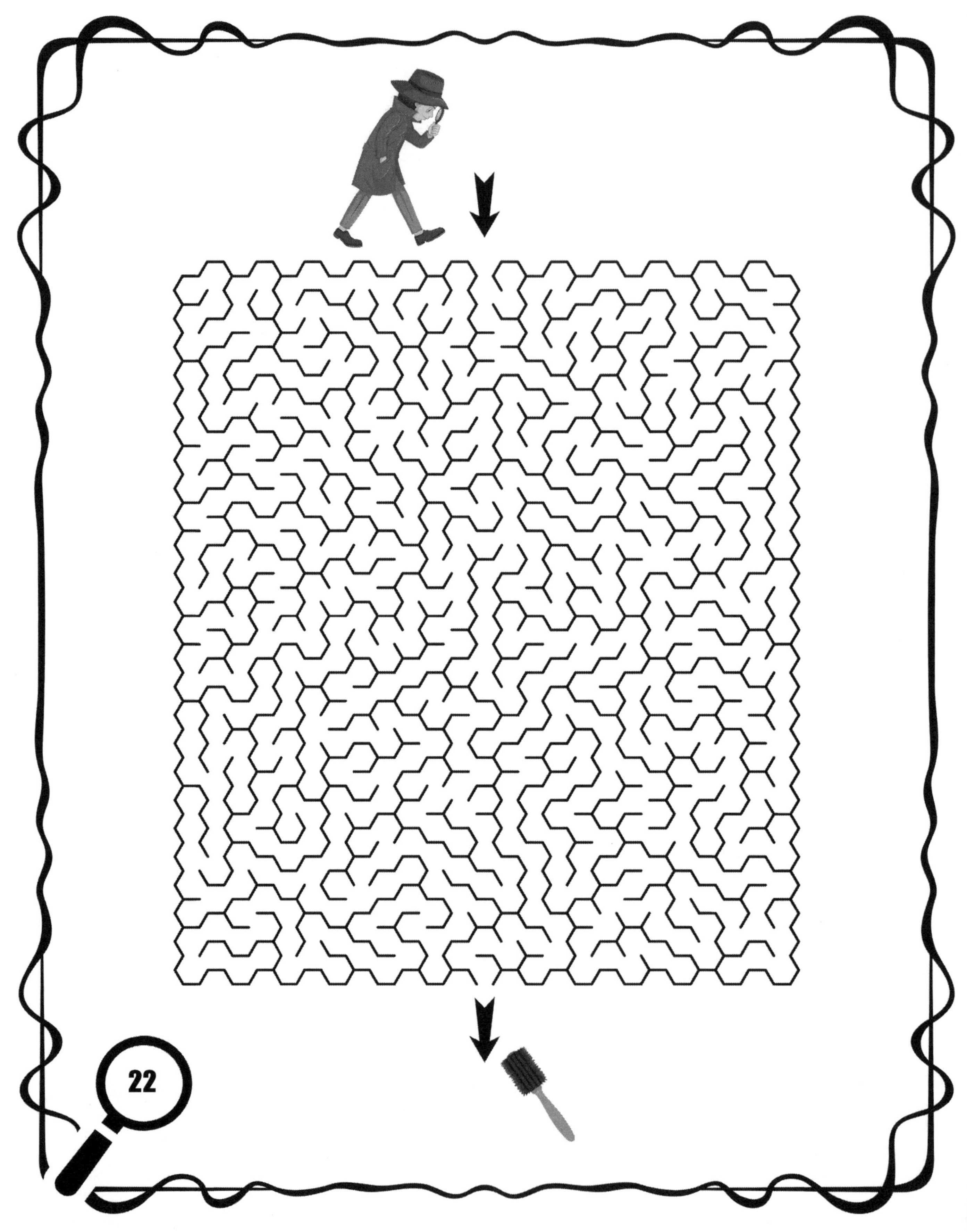

22

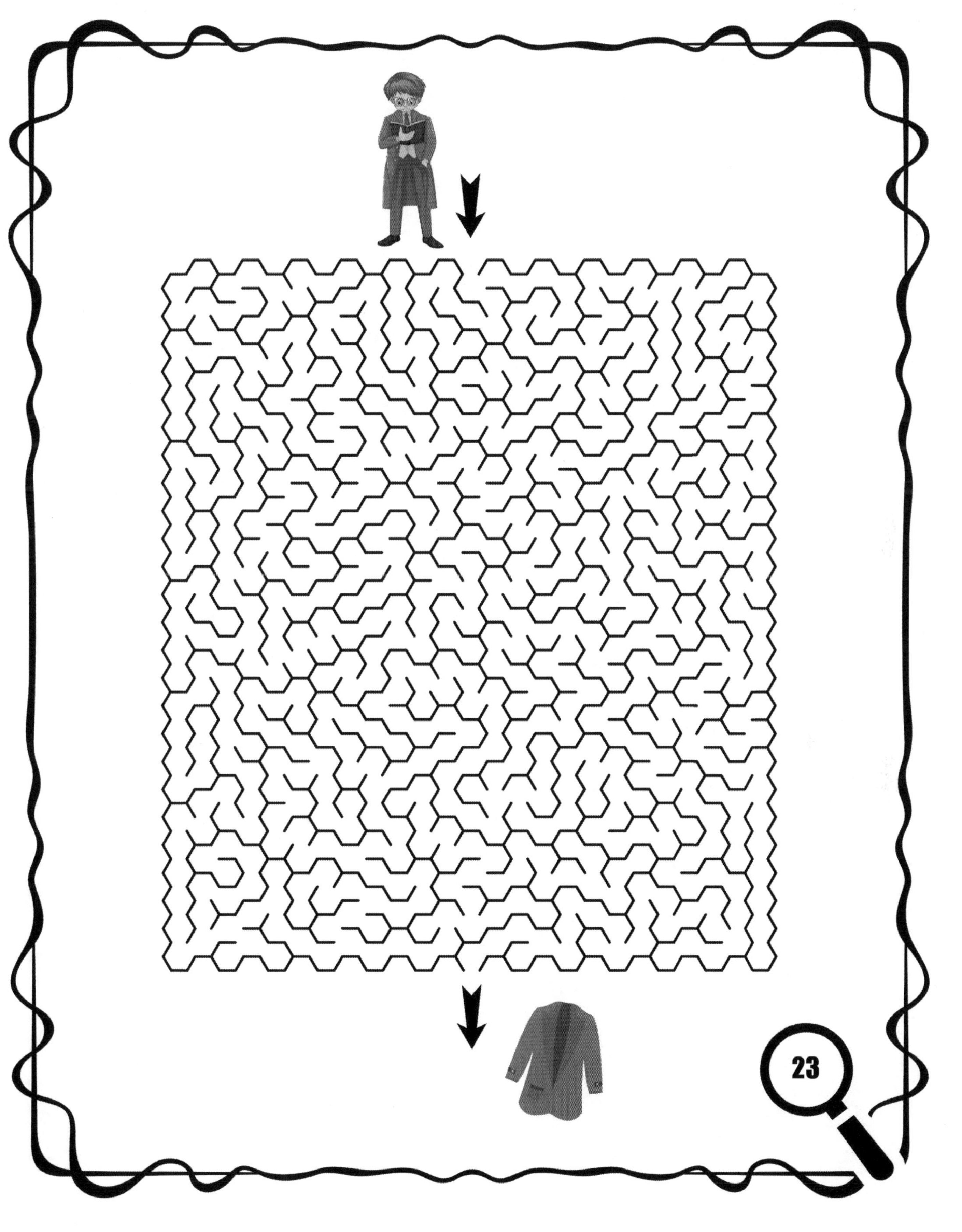

23

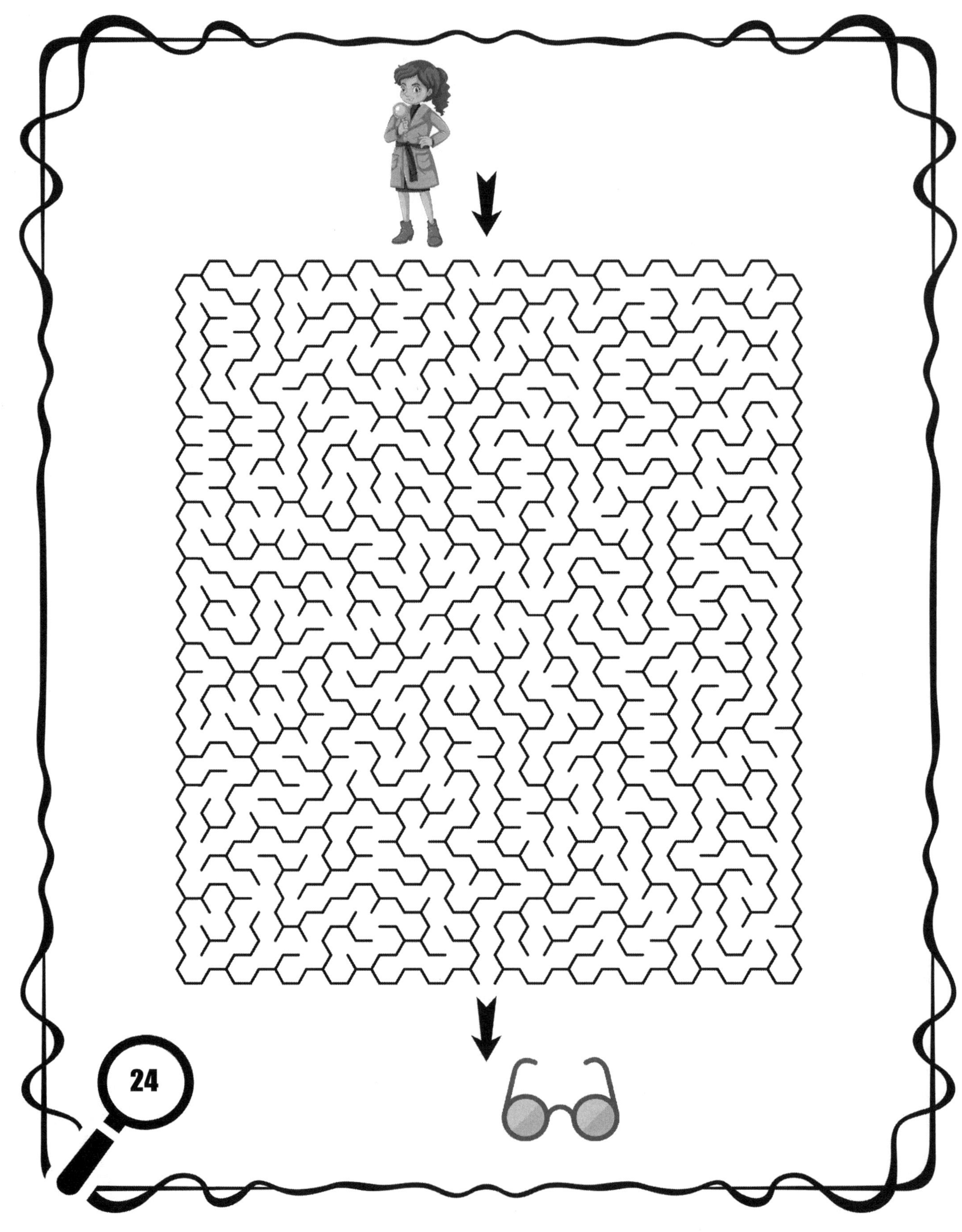

24

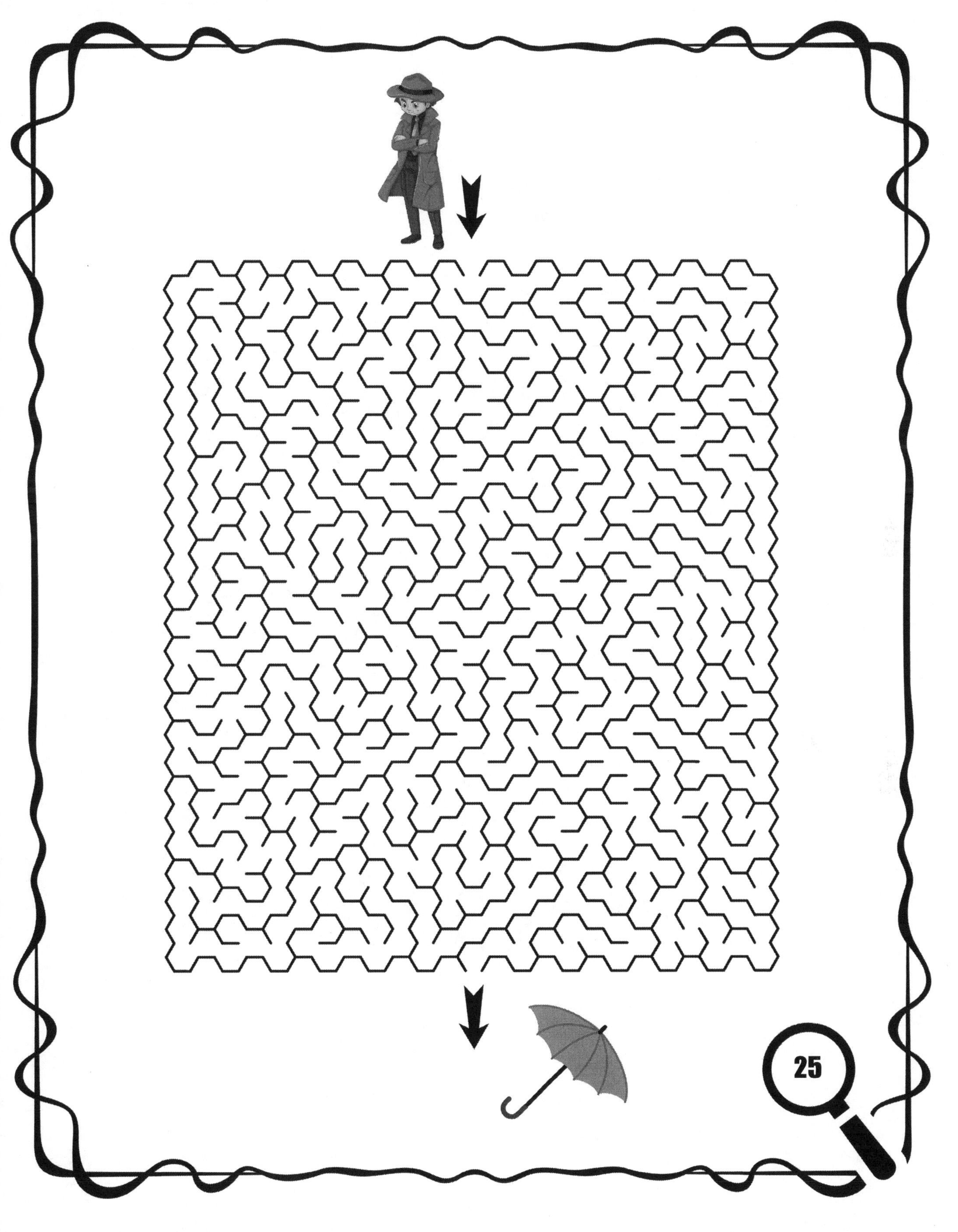

25

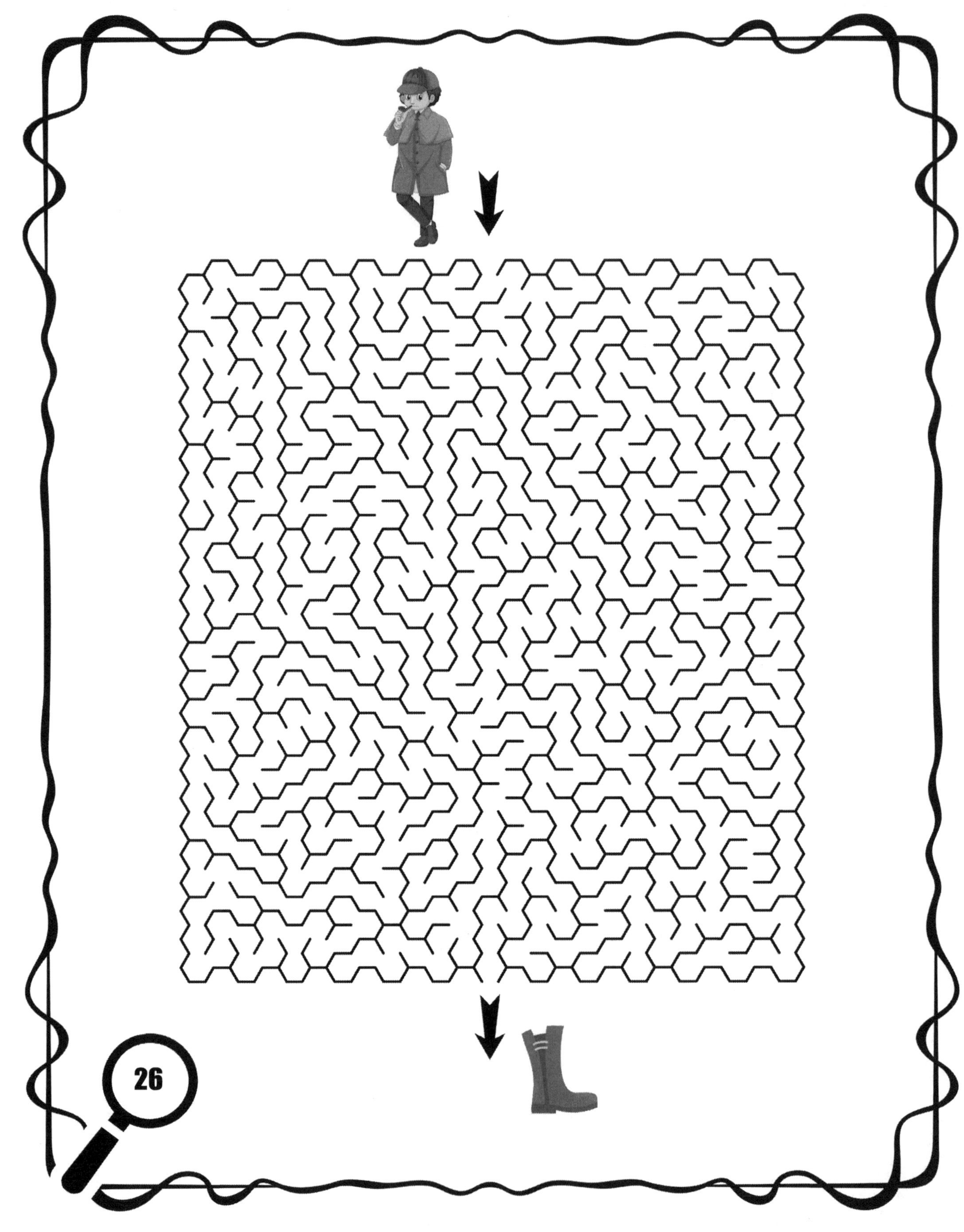

26

27

28

30

32

33

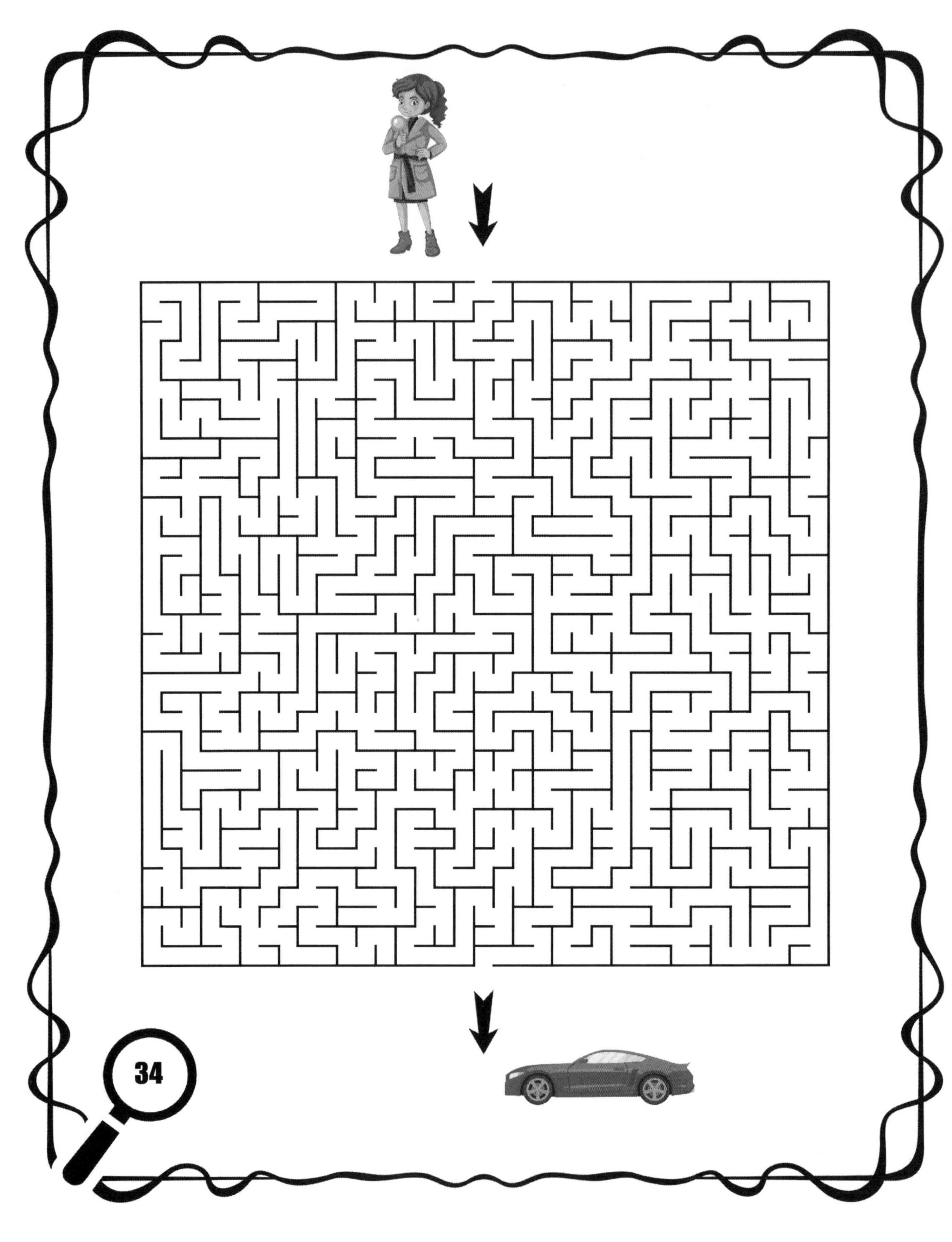

34

35

38

39

40

43

44

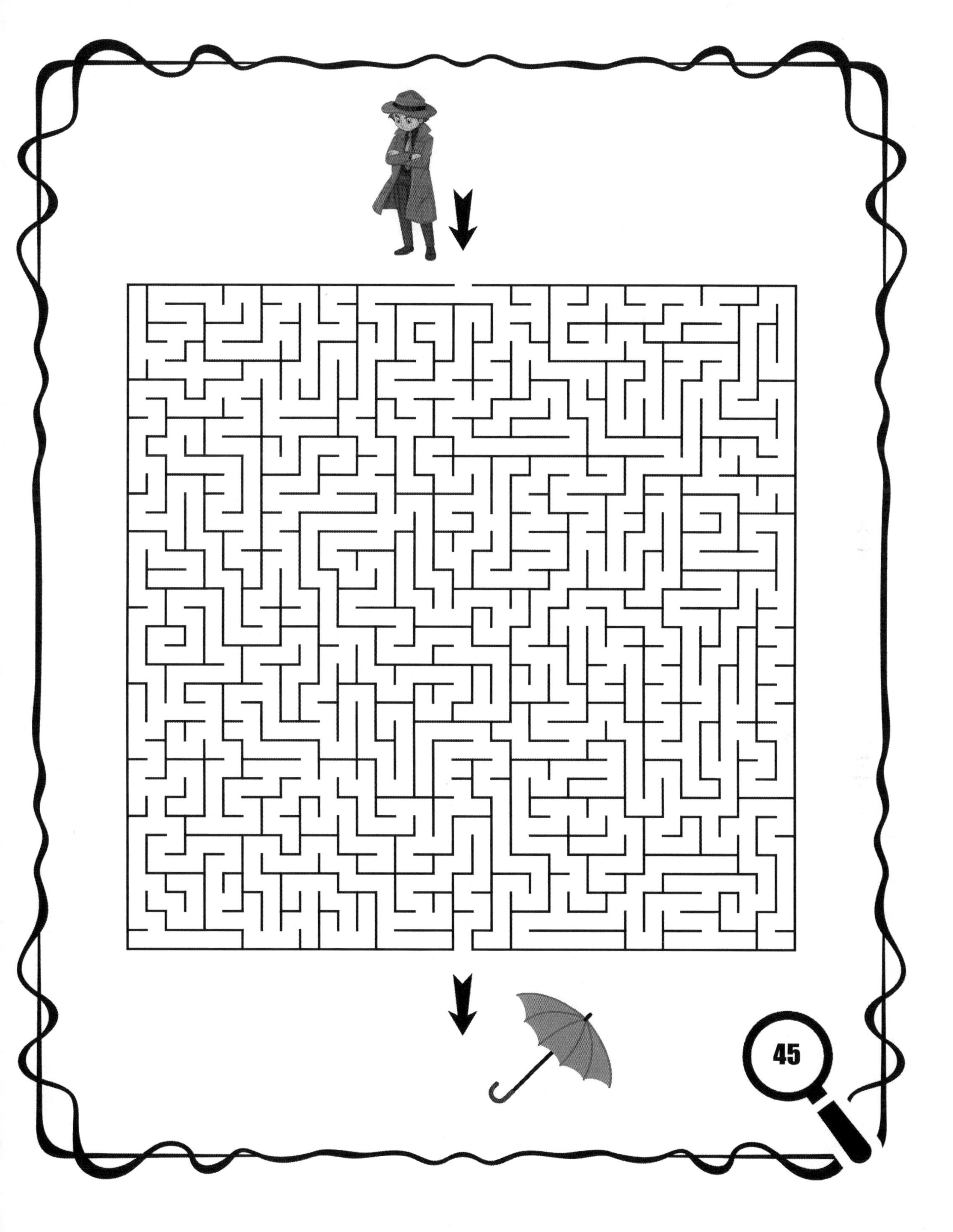

45

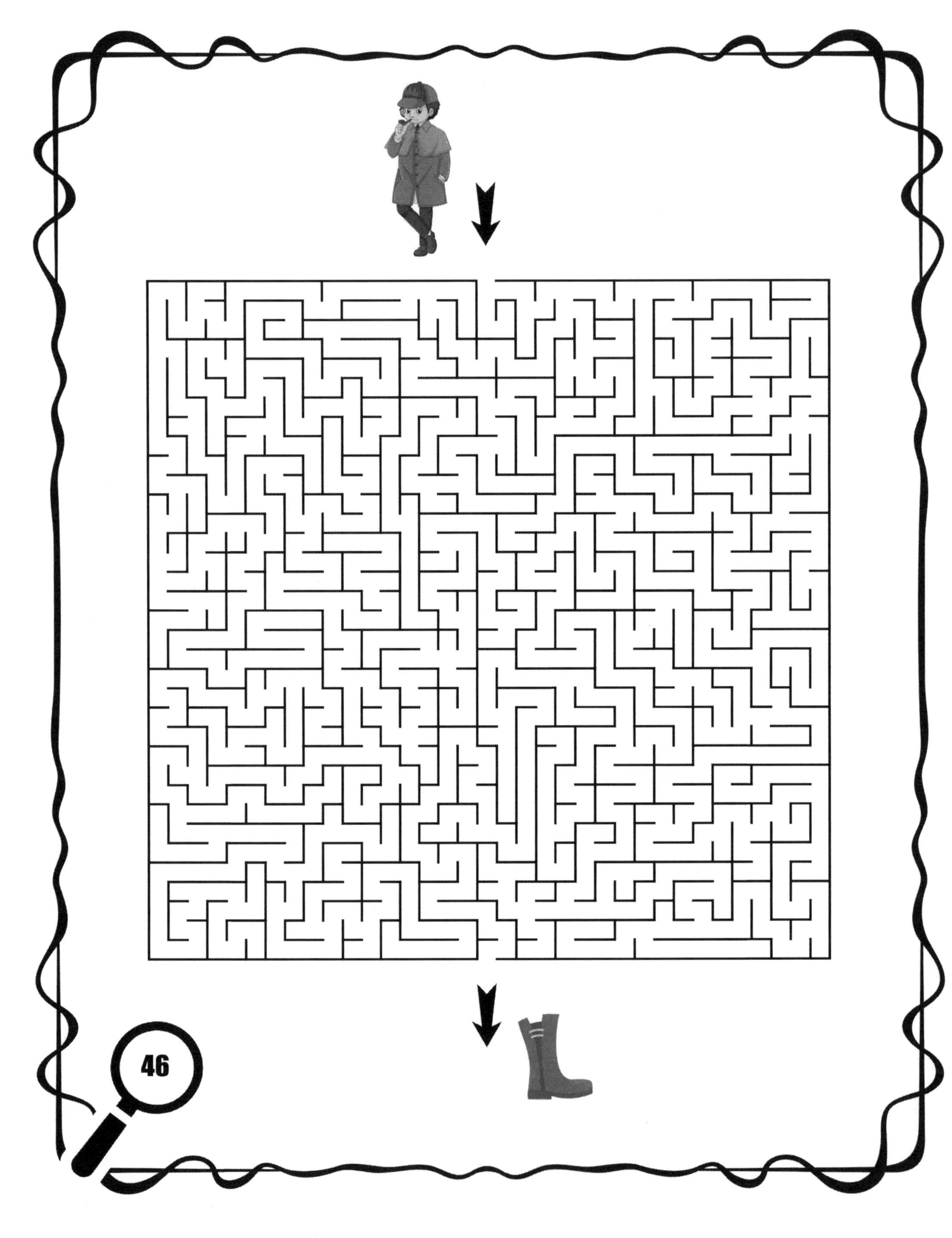

47

49

50

51

53

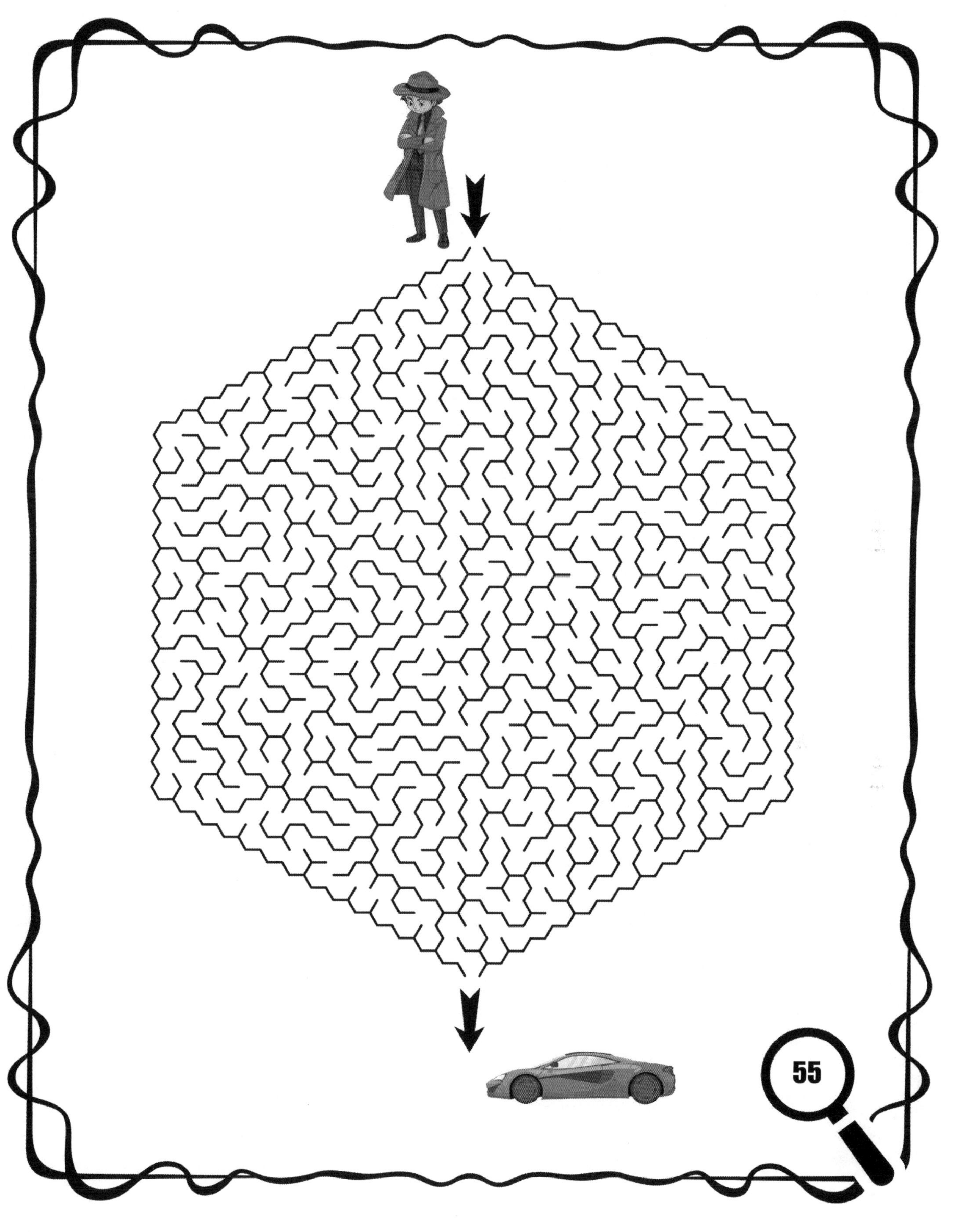

55

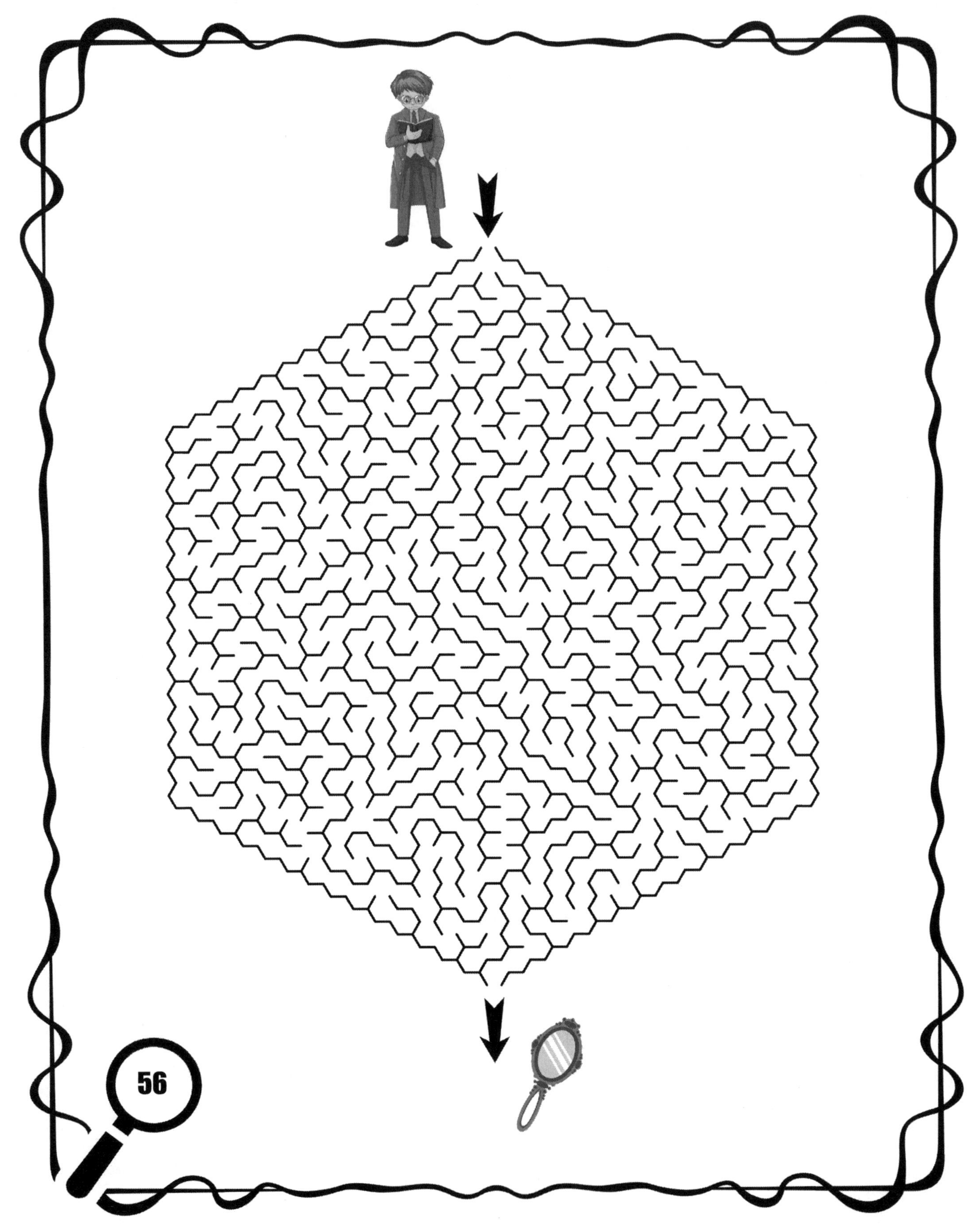

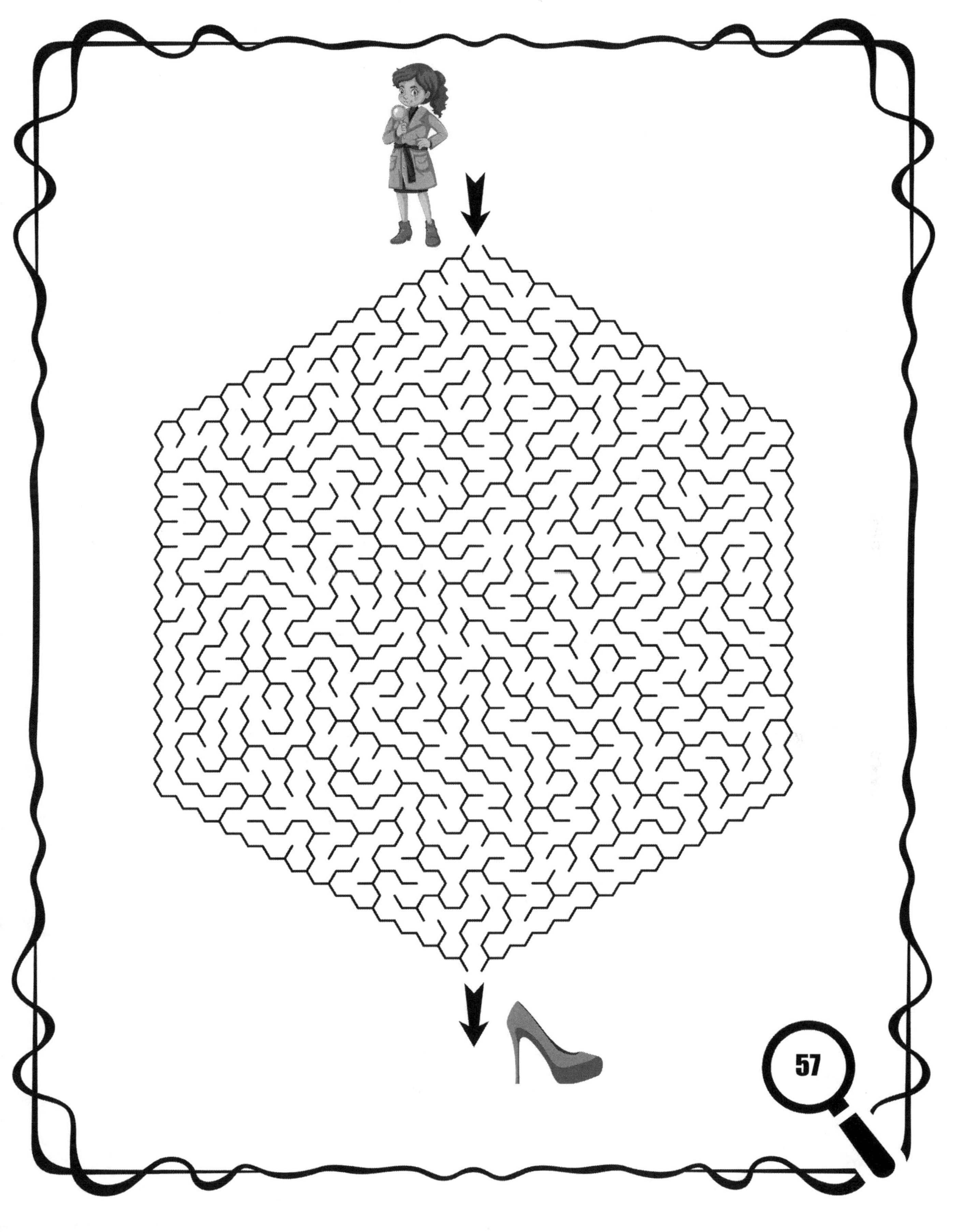

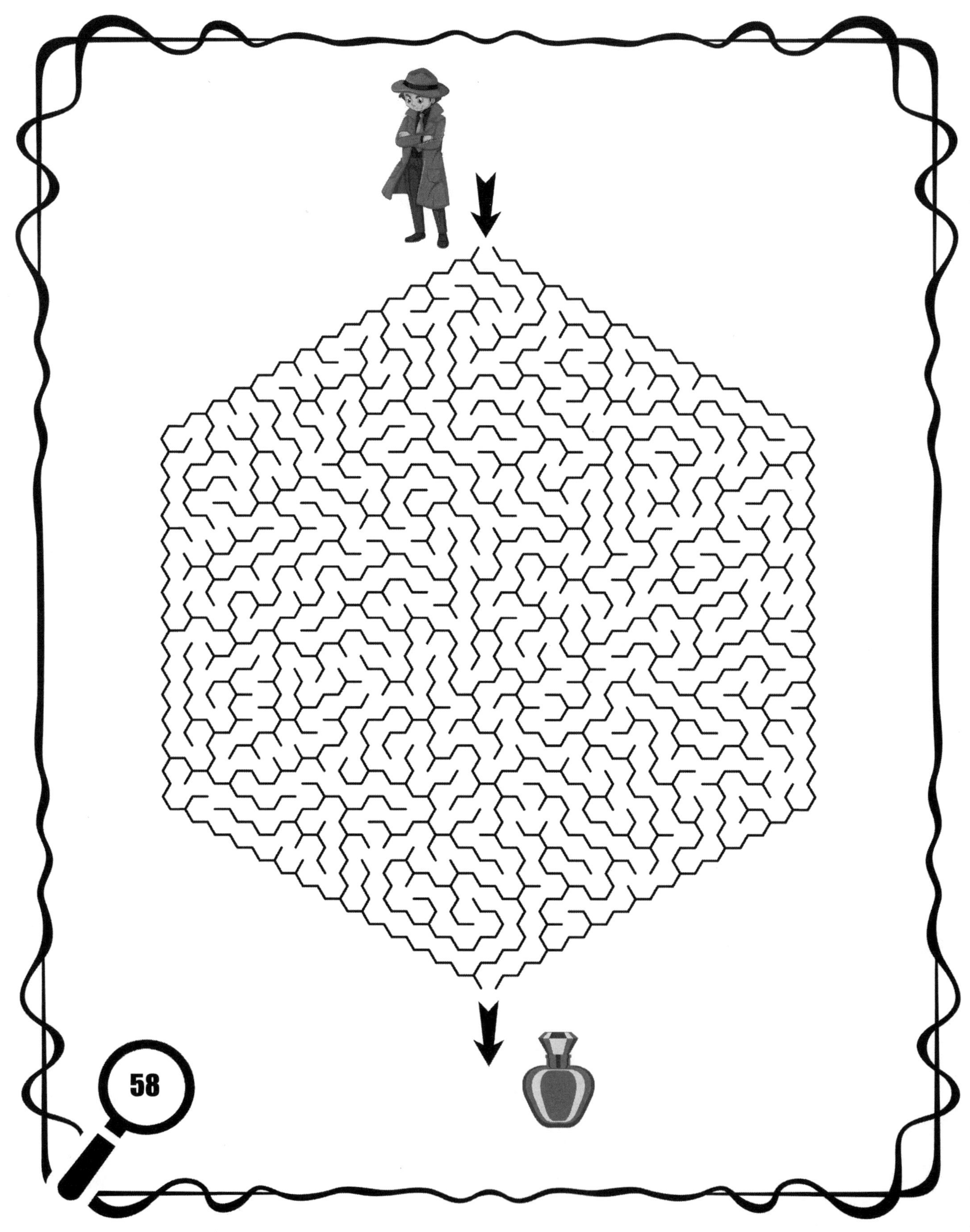

58

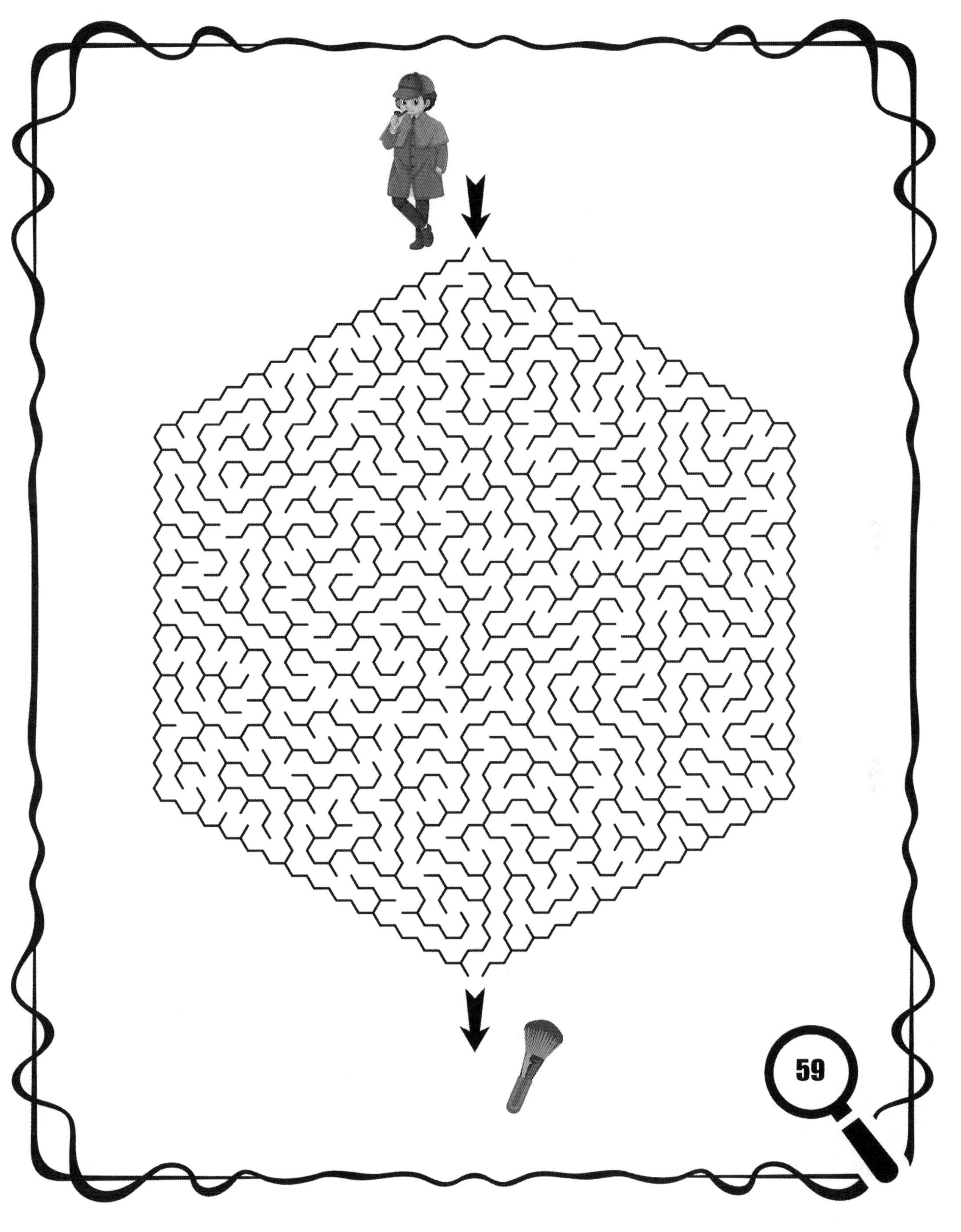

59

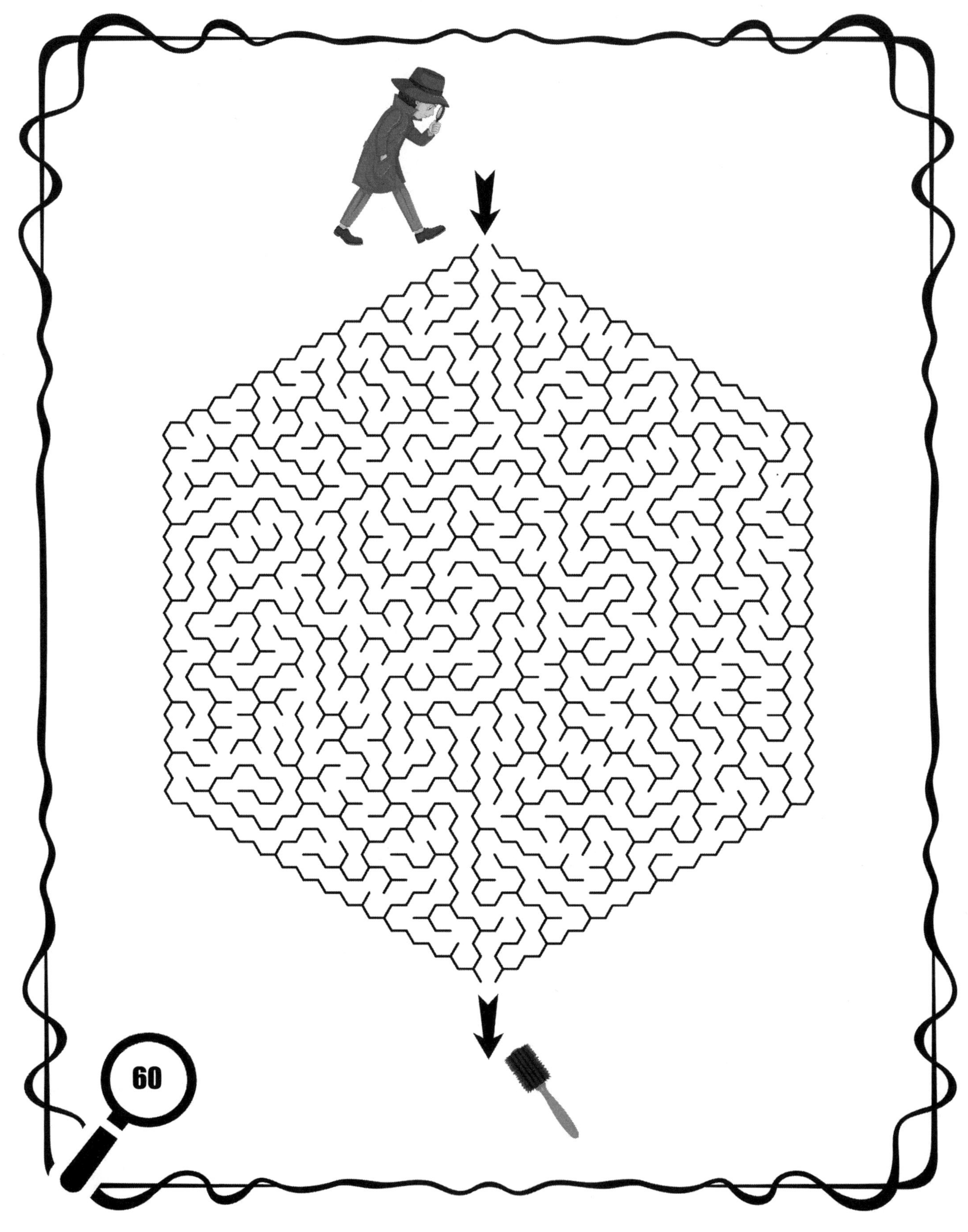

60

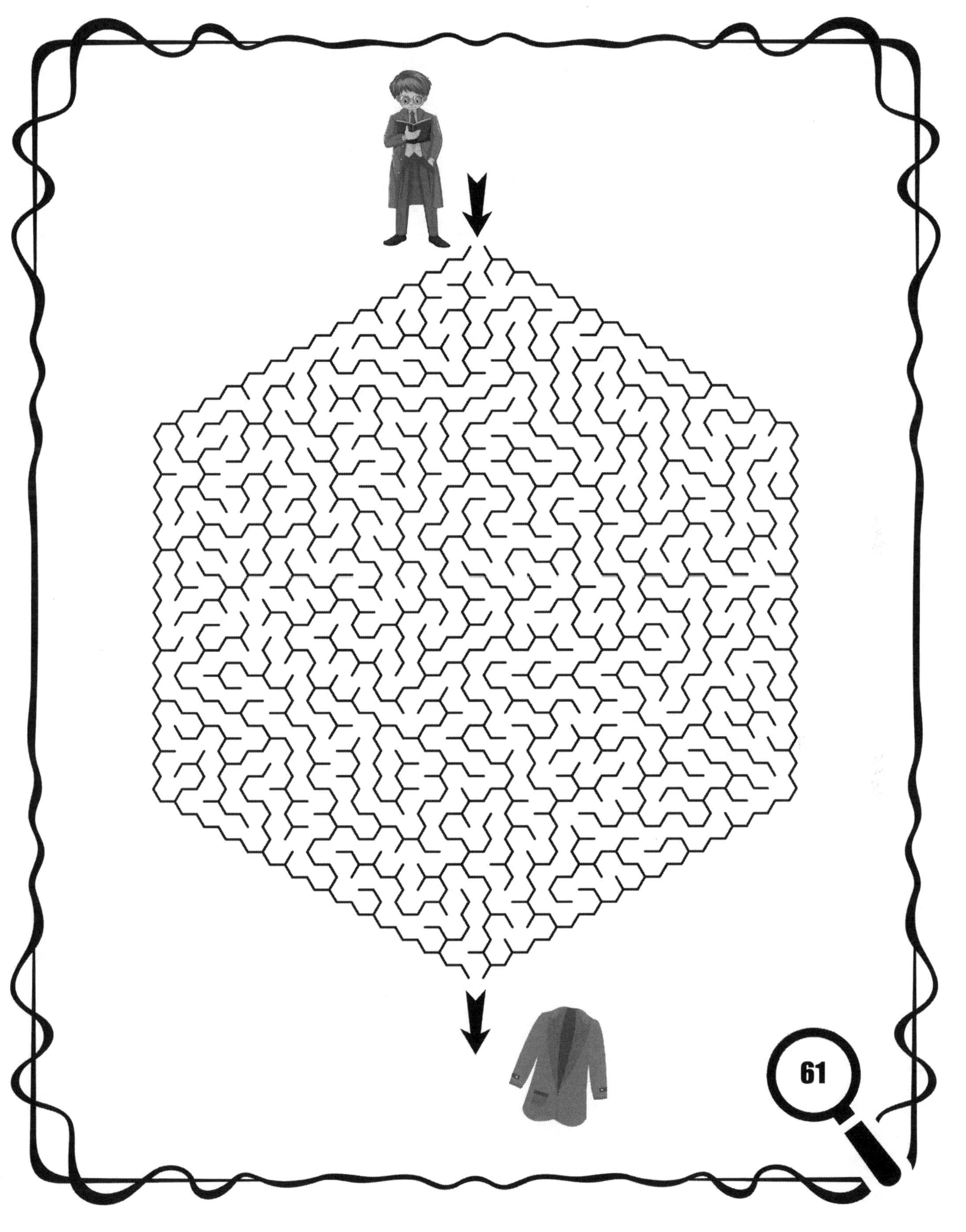

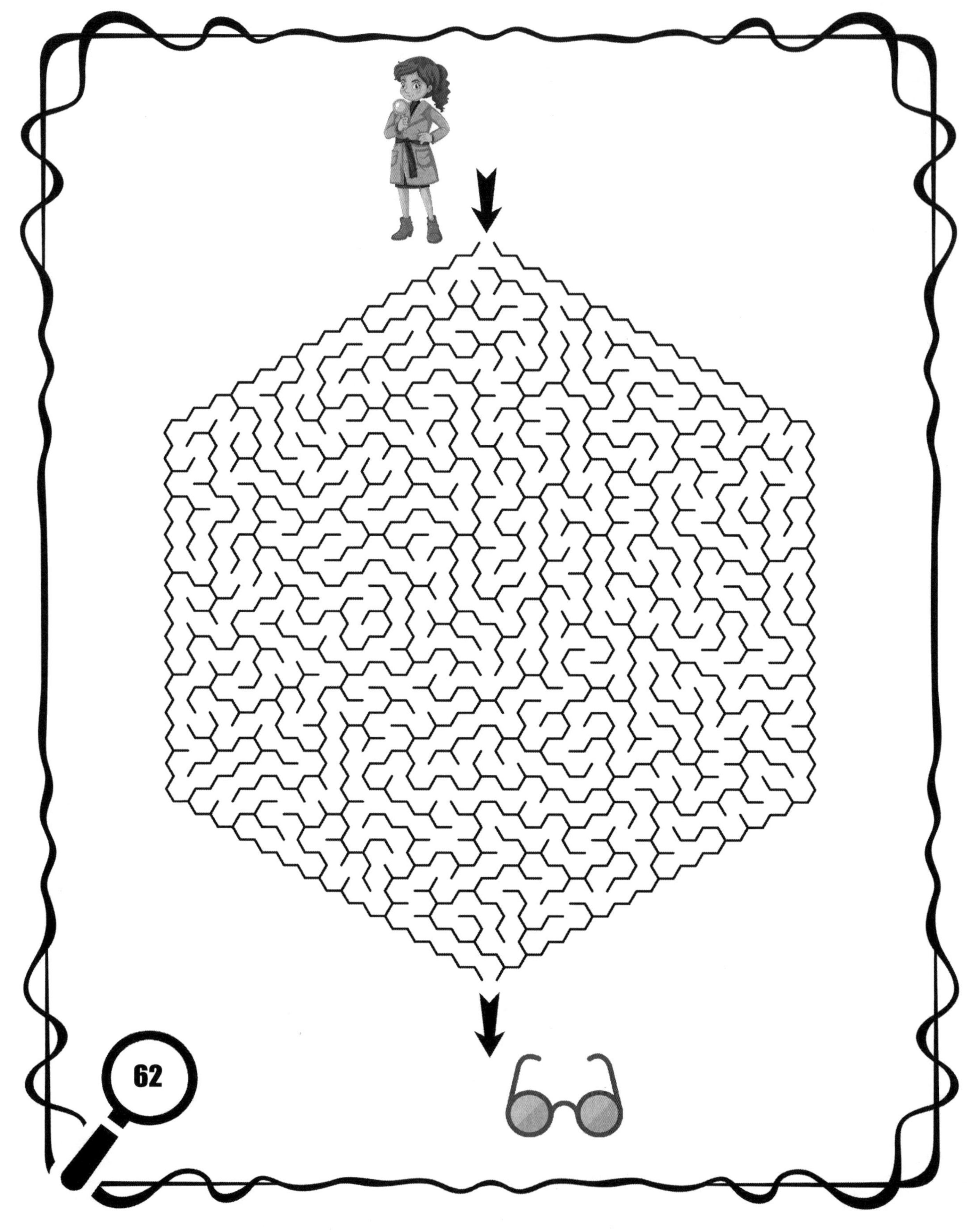

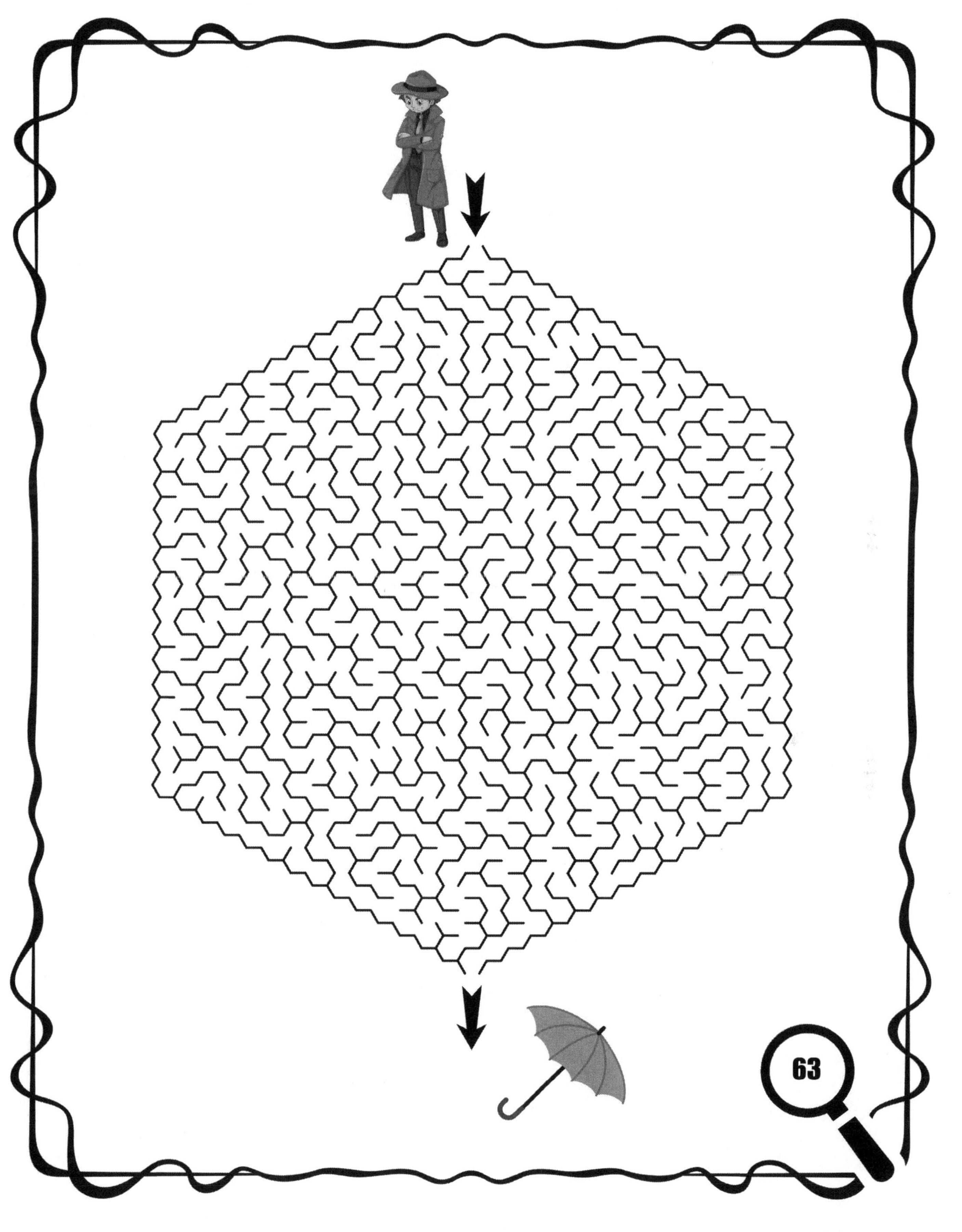

63

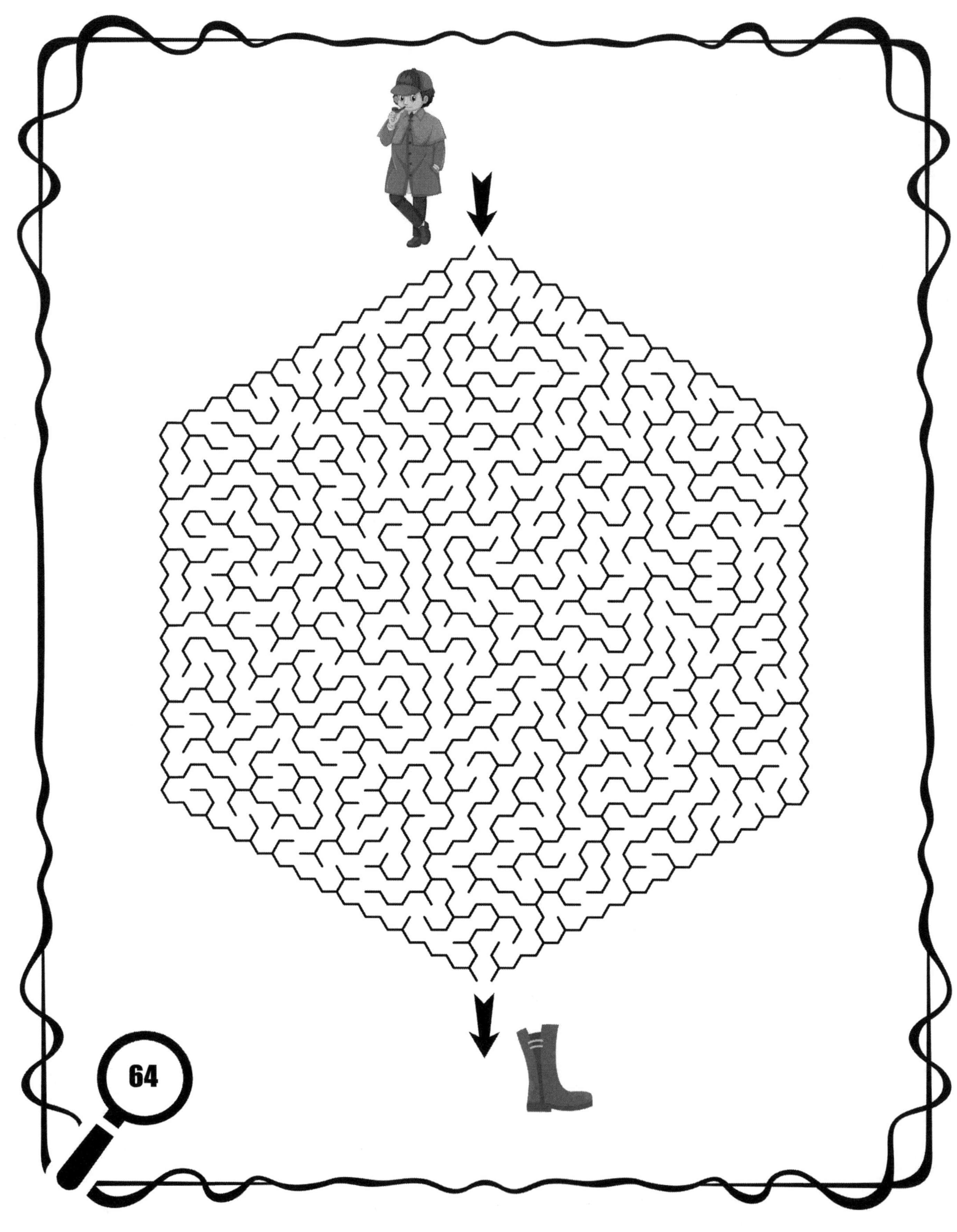

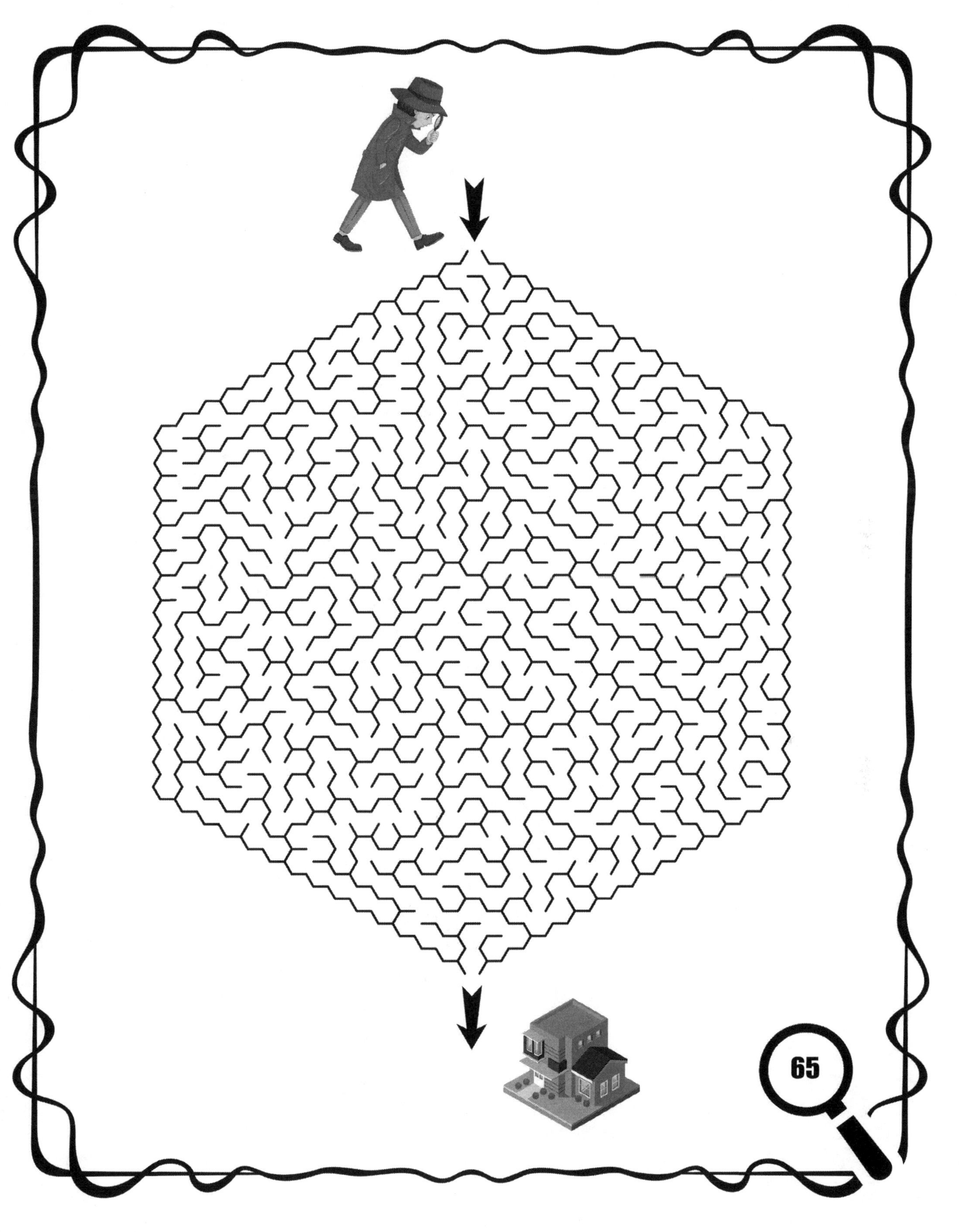

65

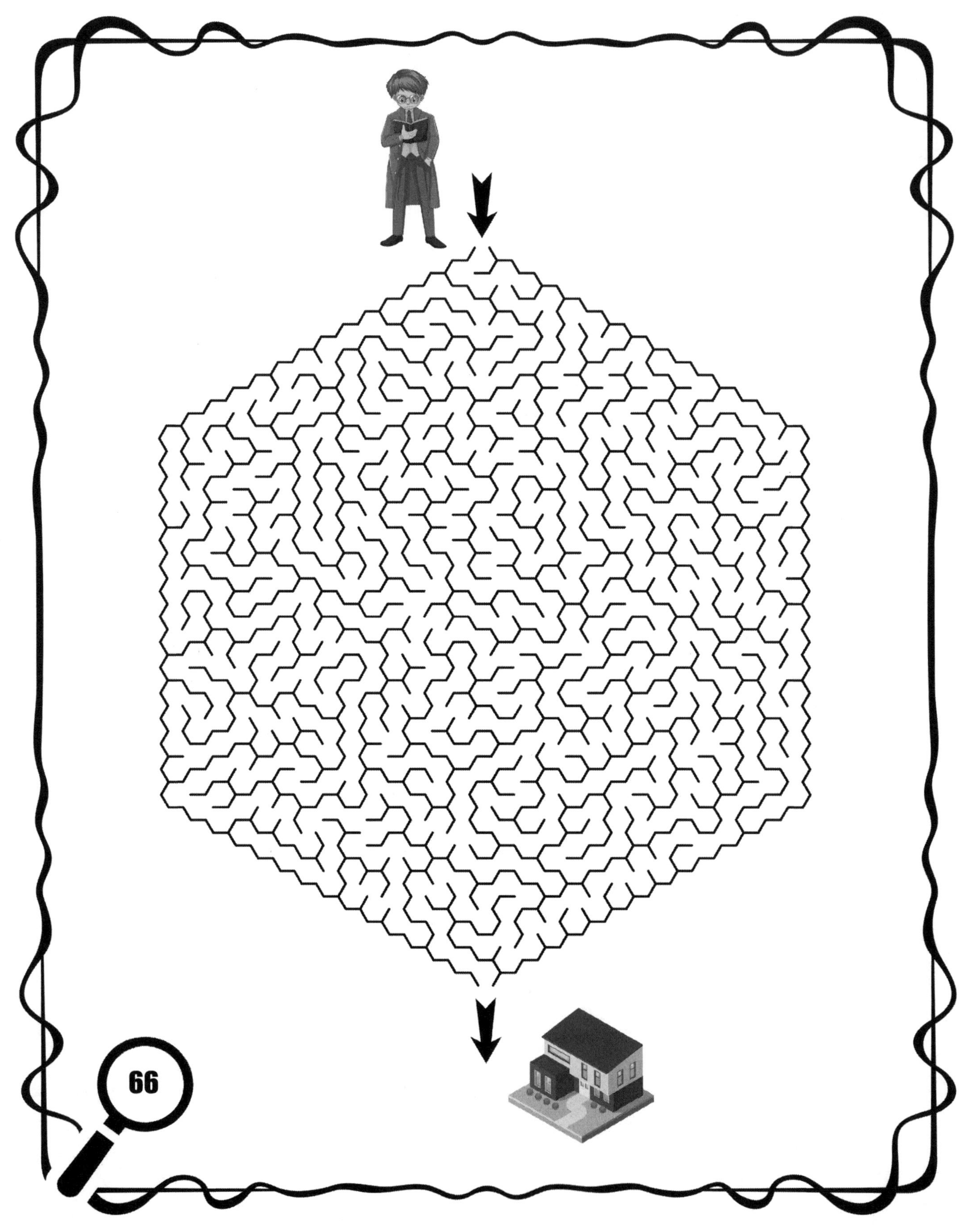

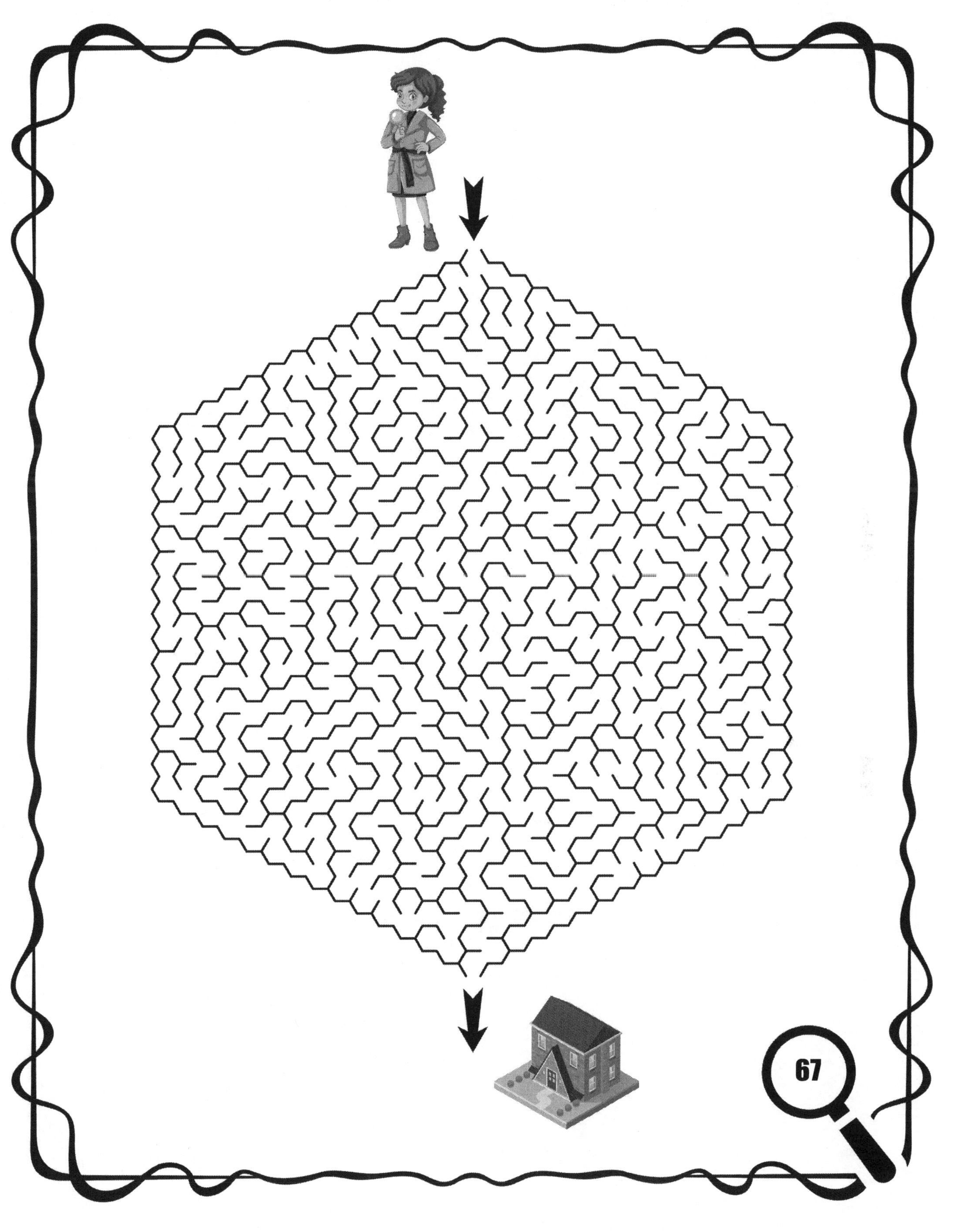

67

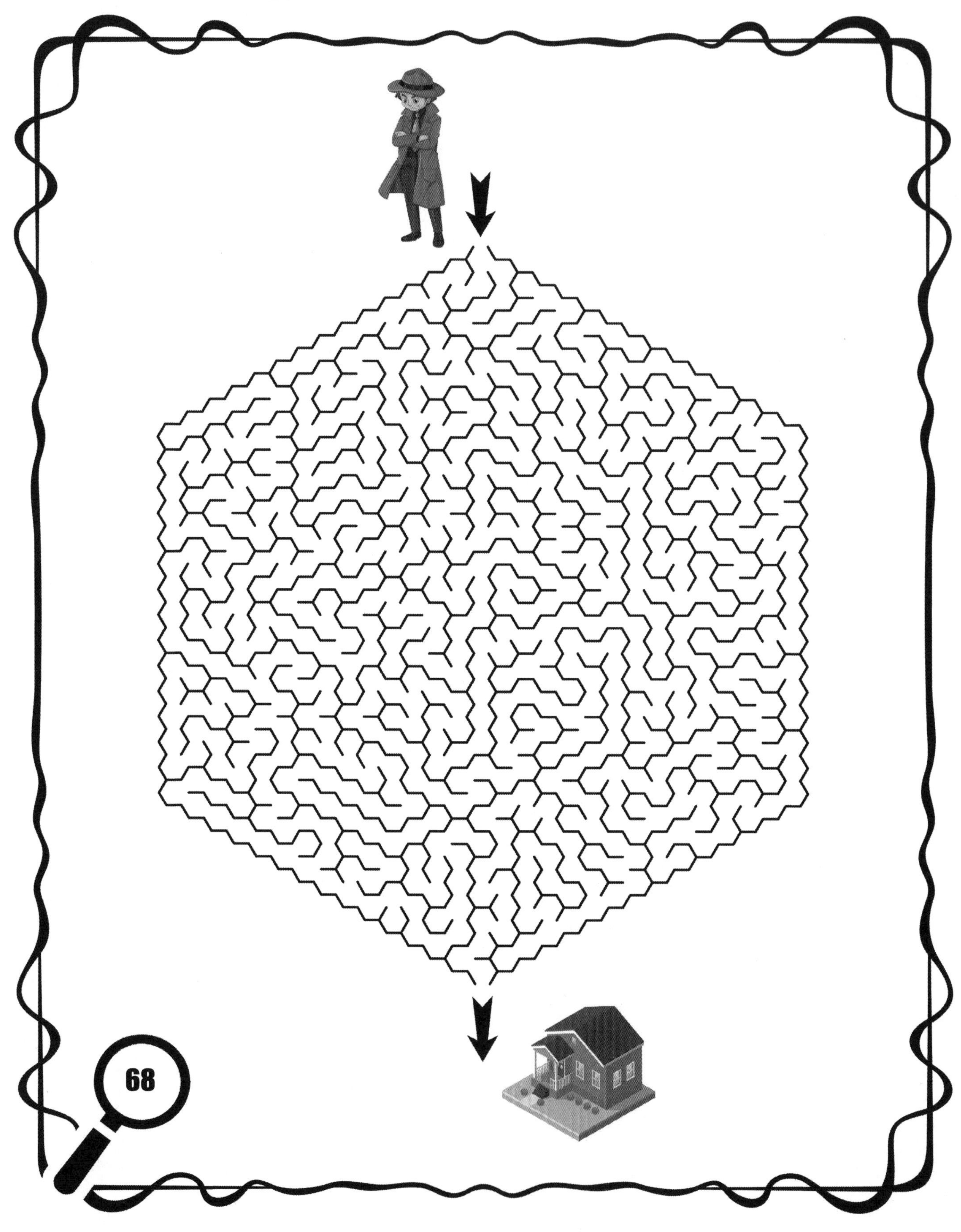

68

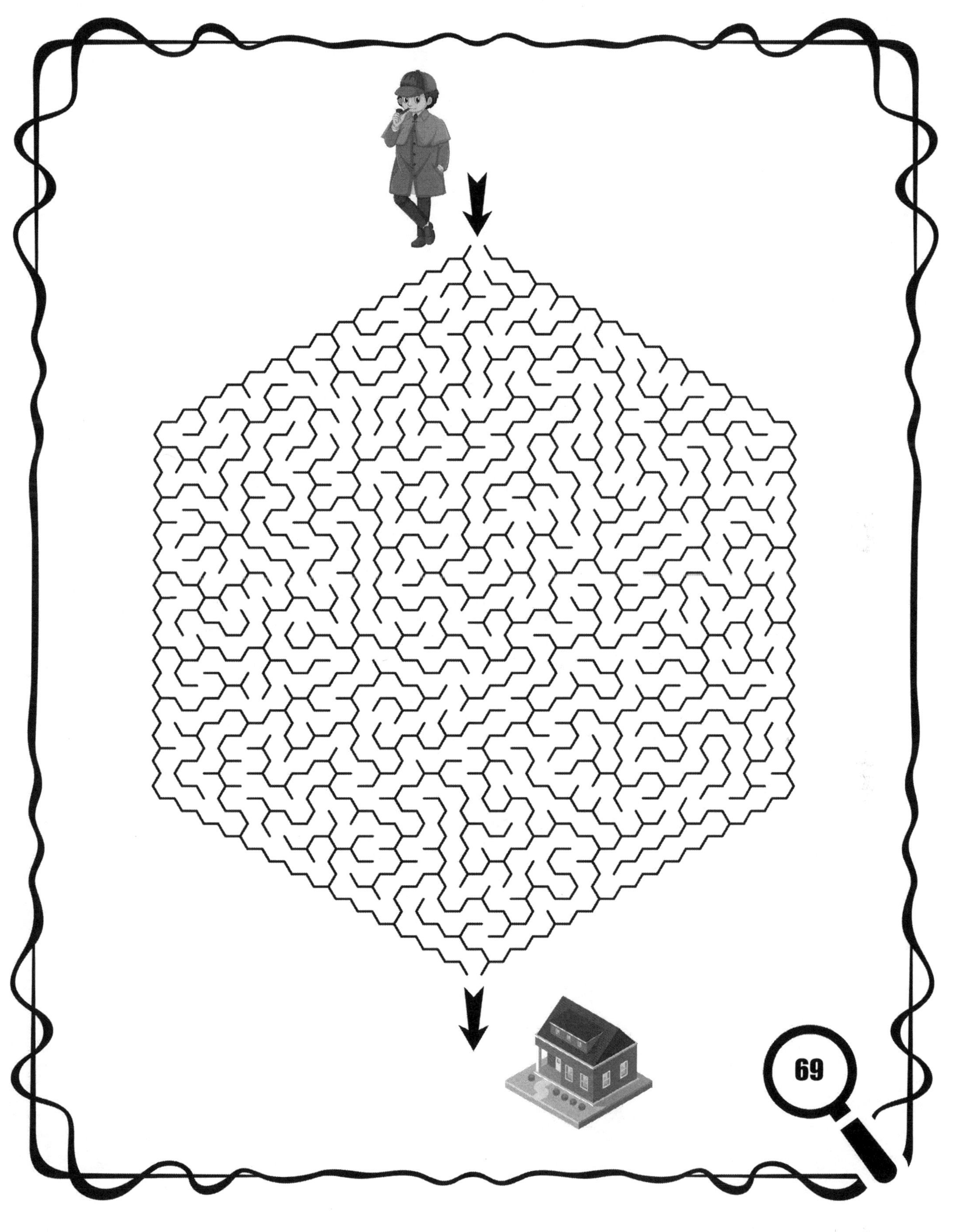

69

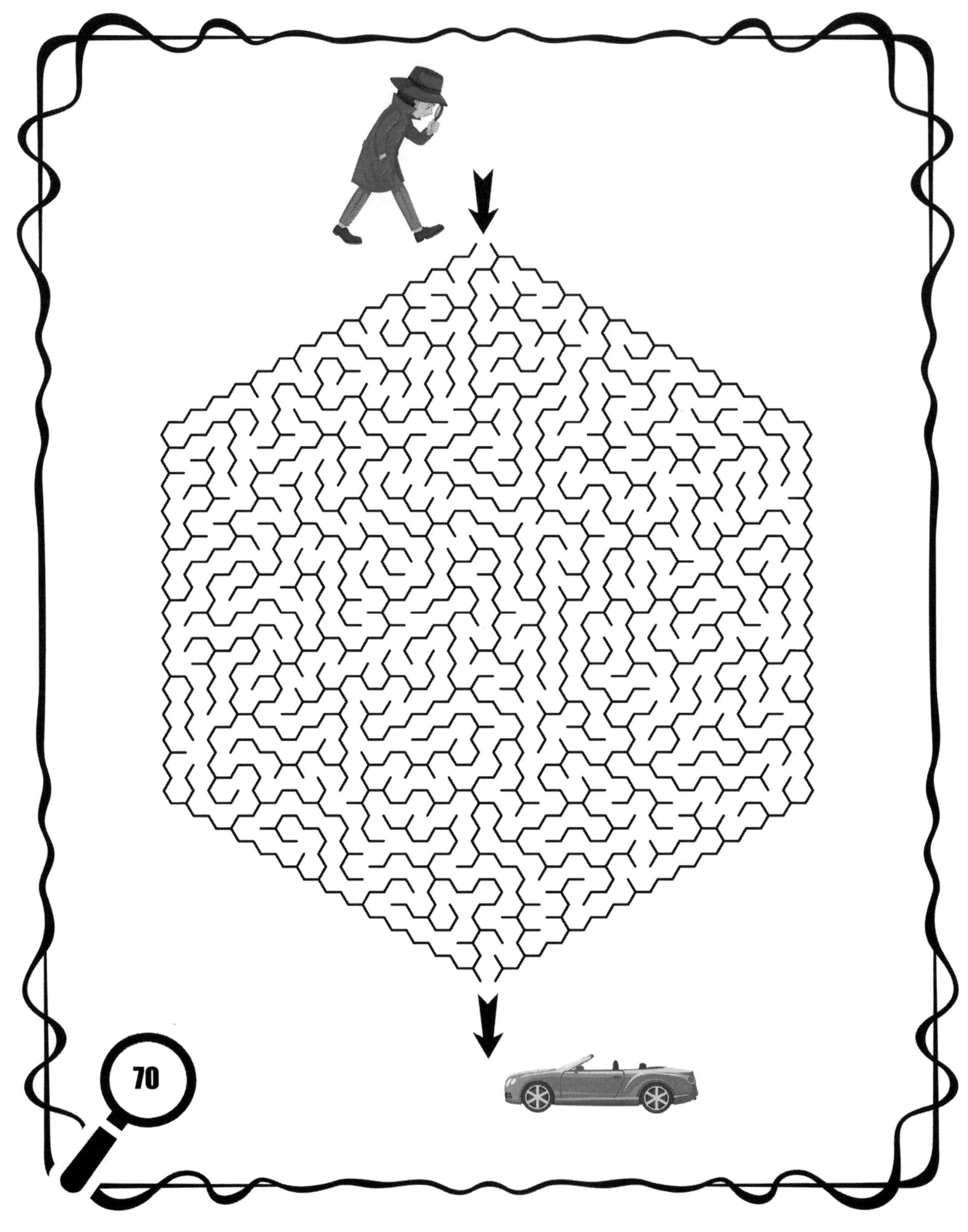

70

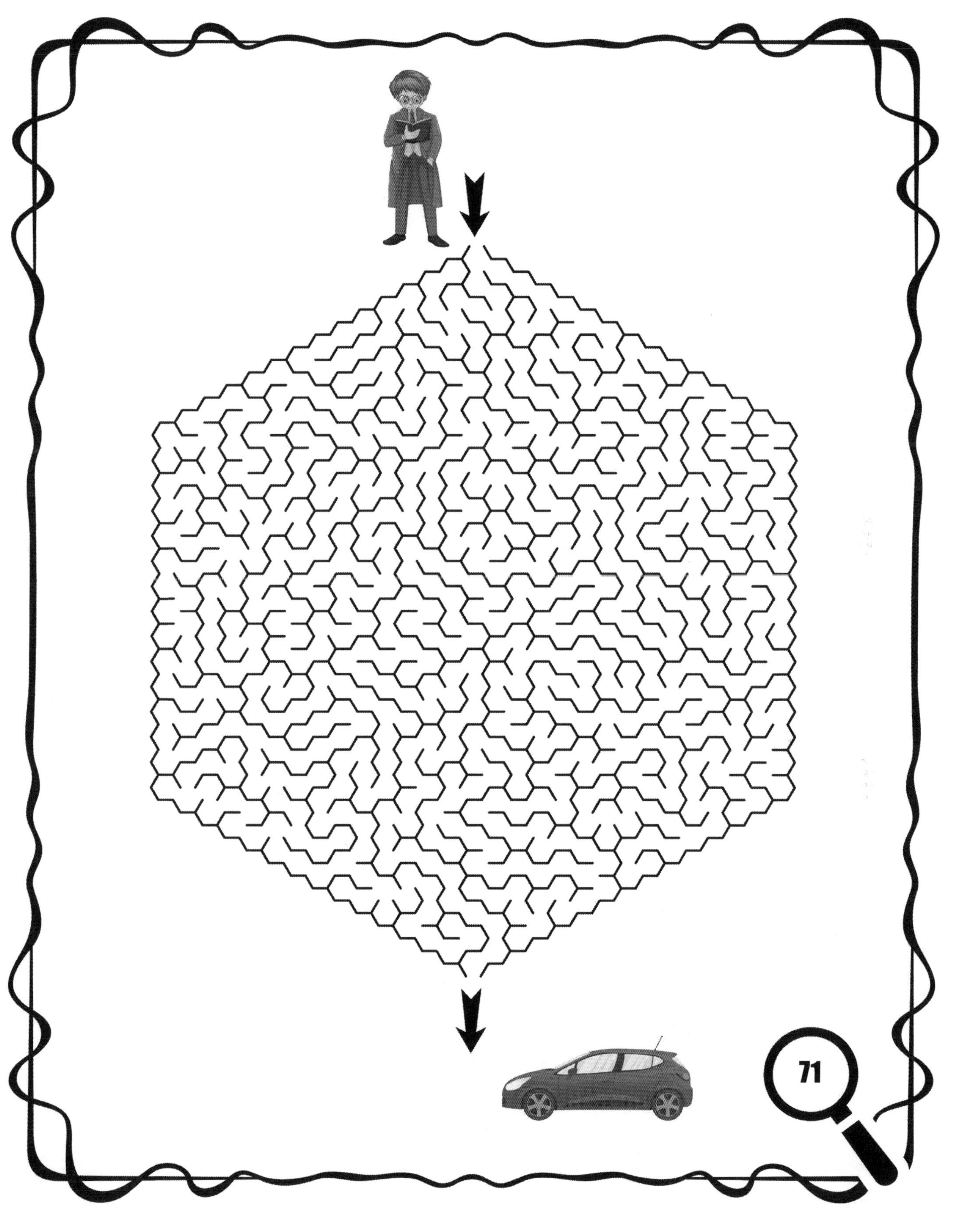

71

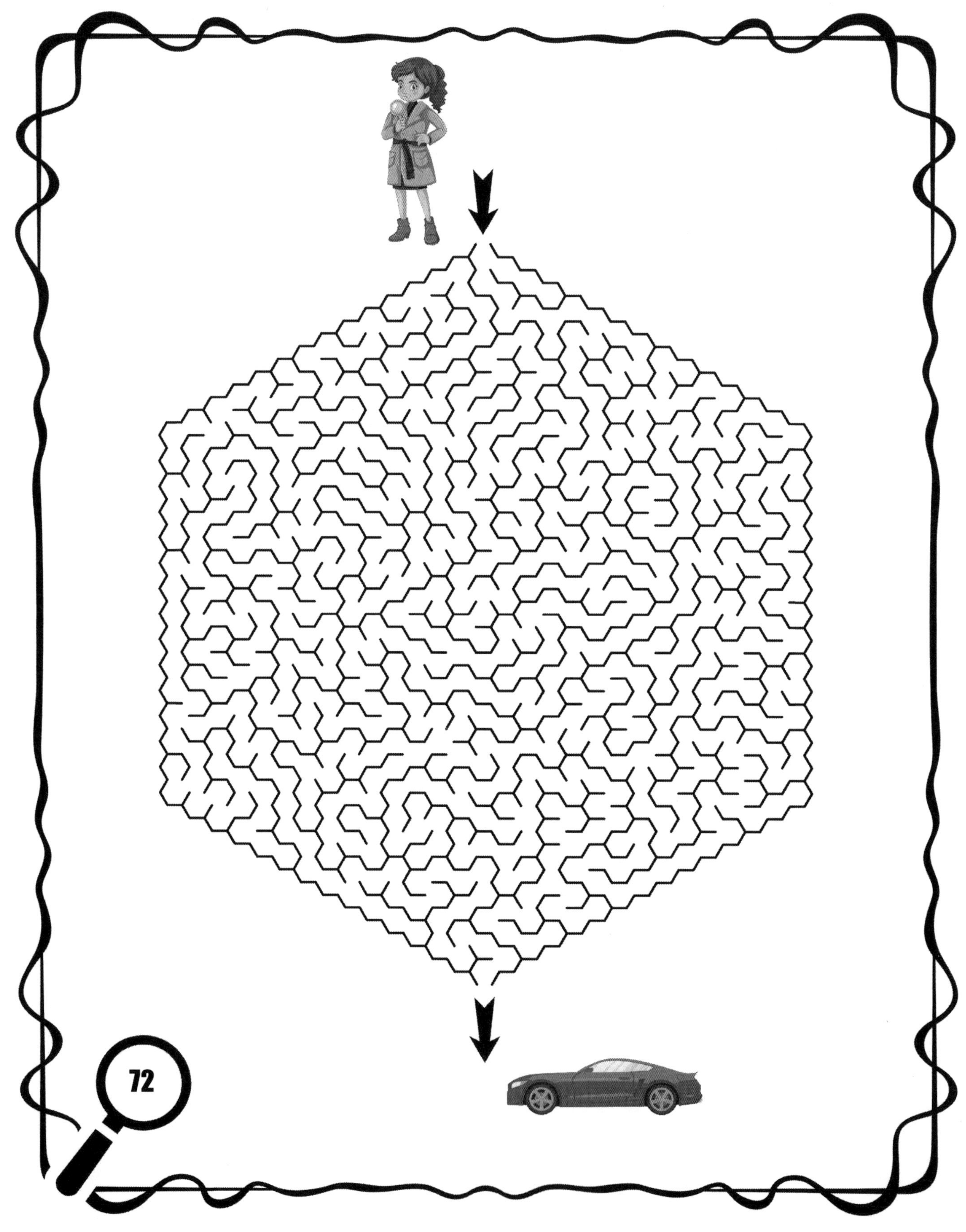

72

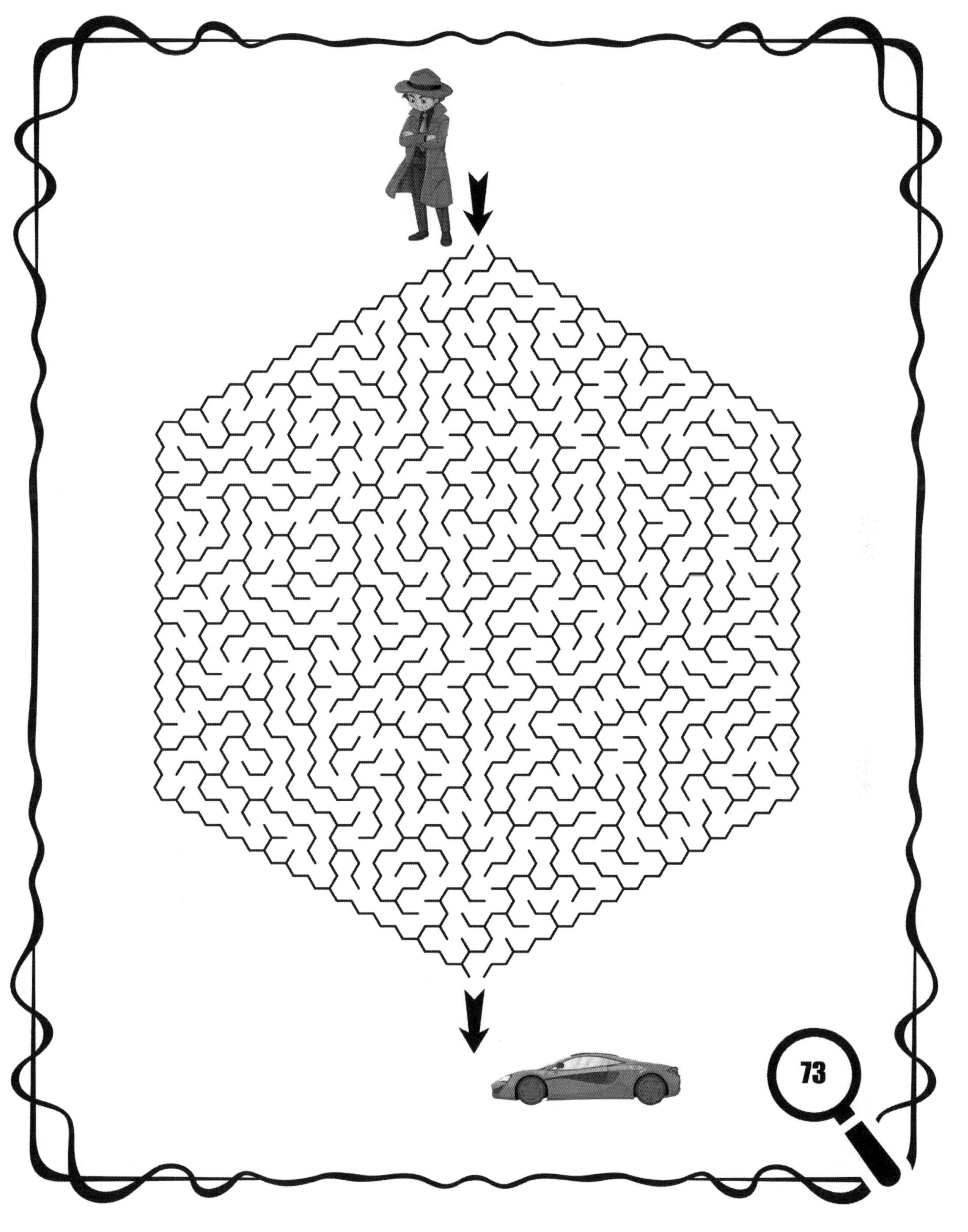

73

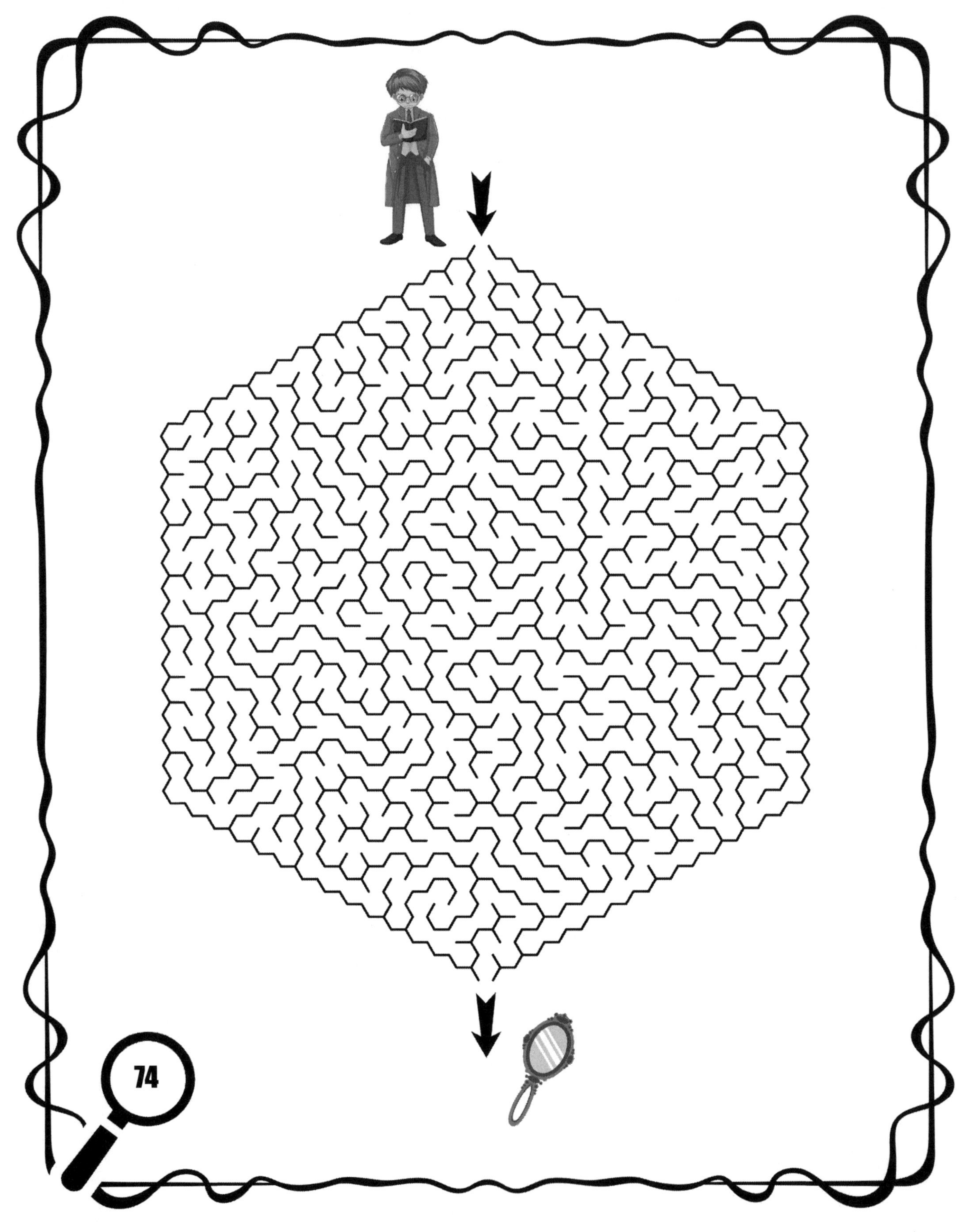

74

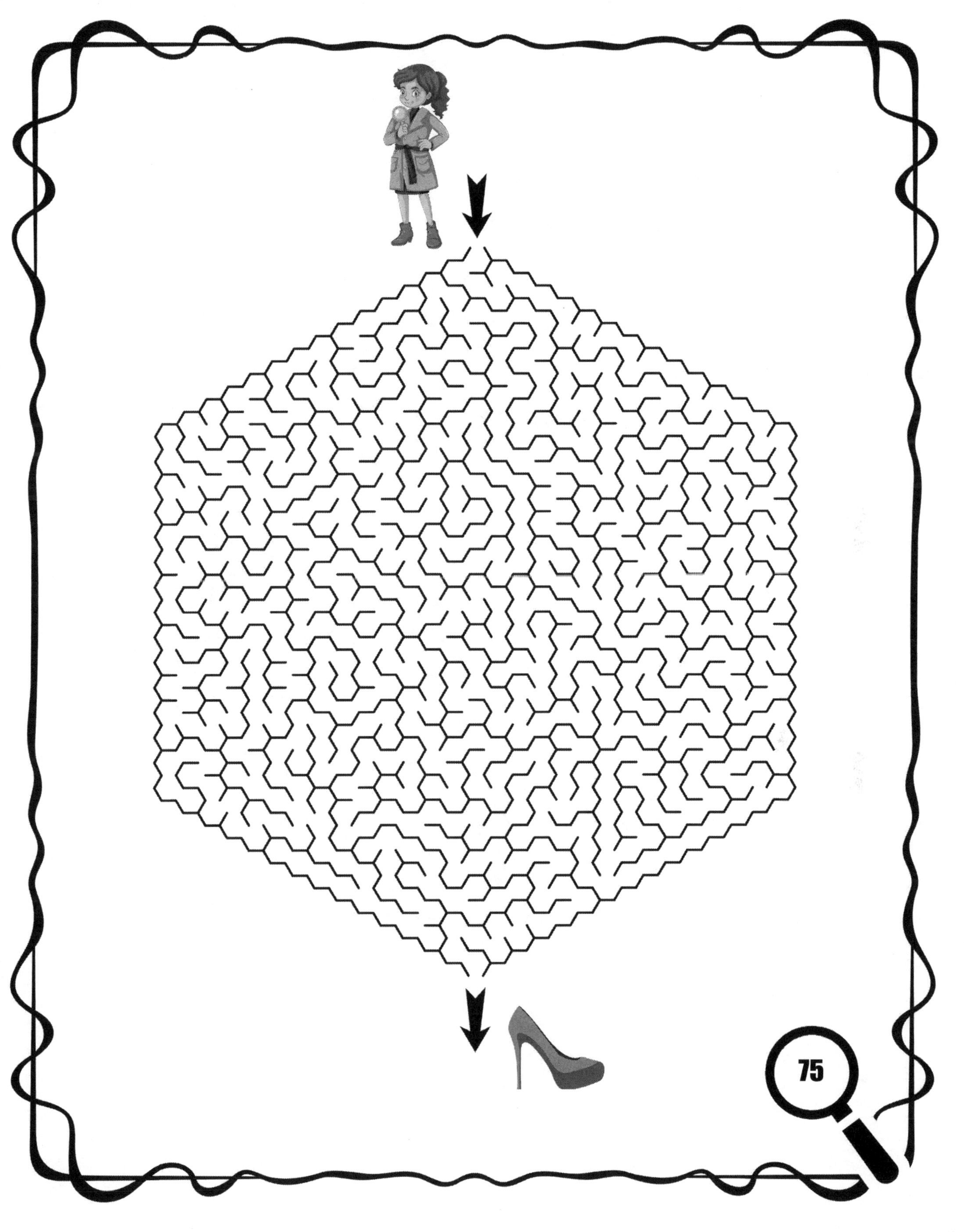

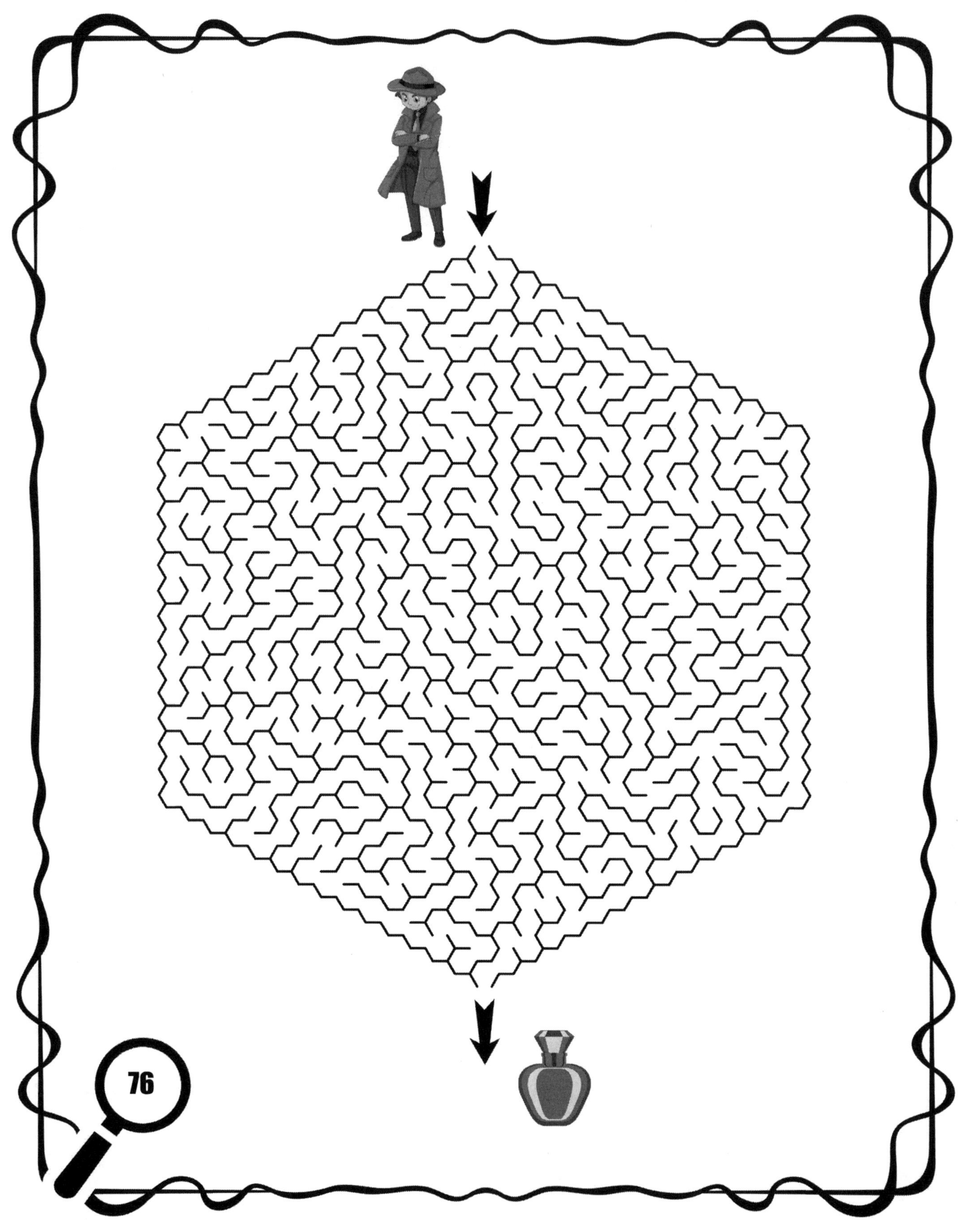

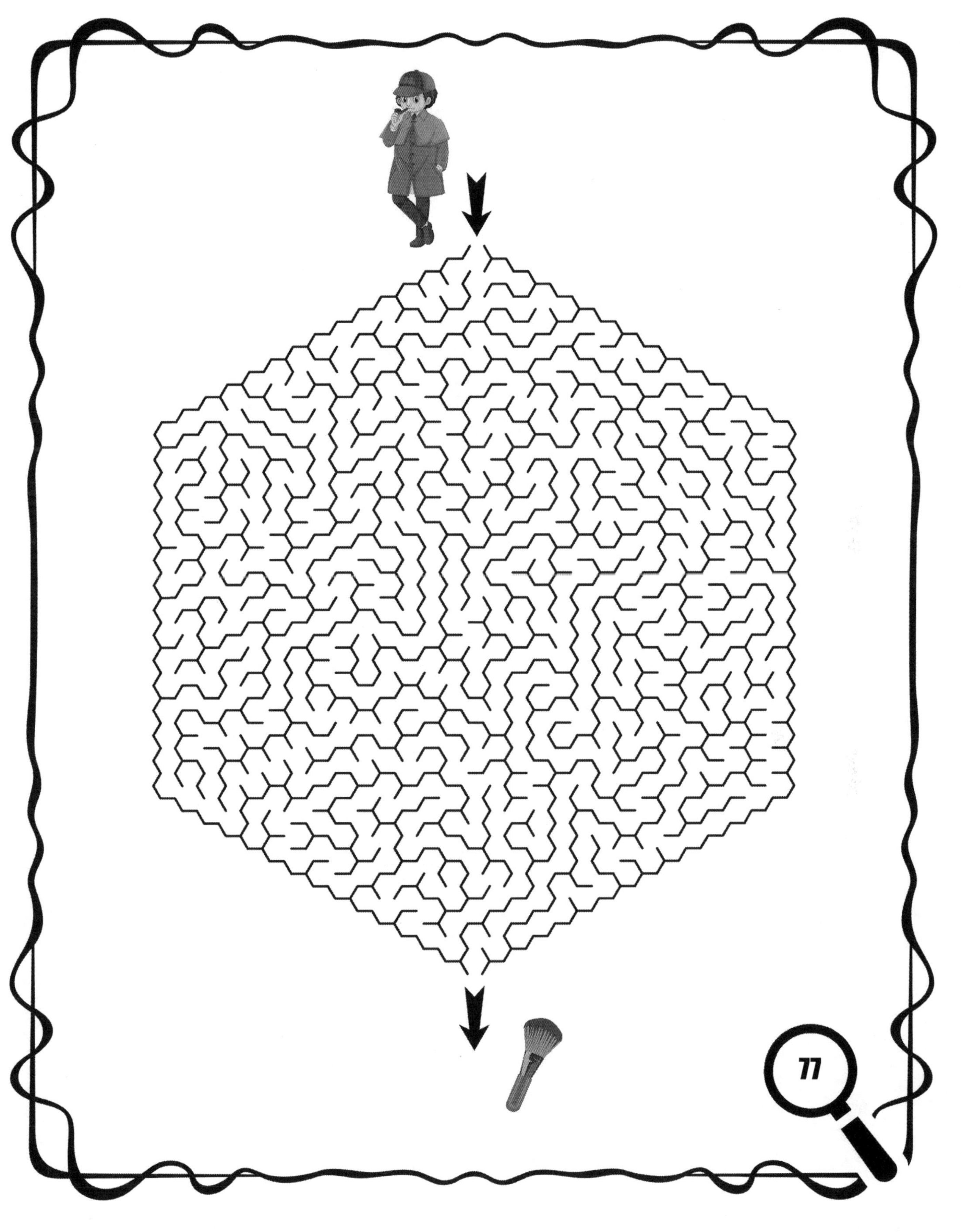

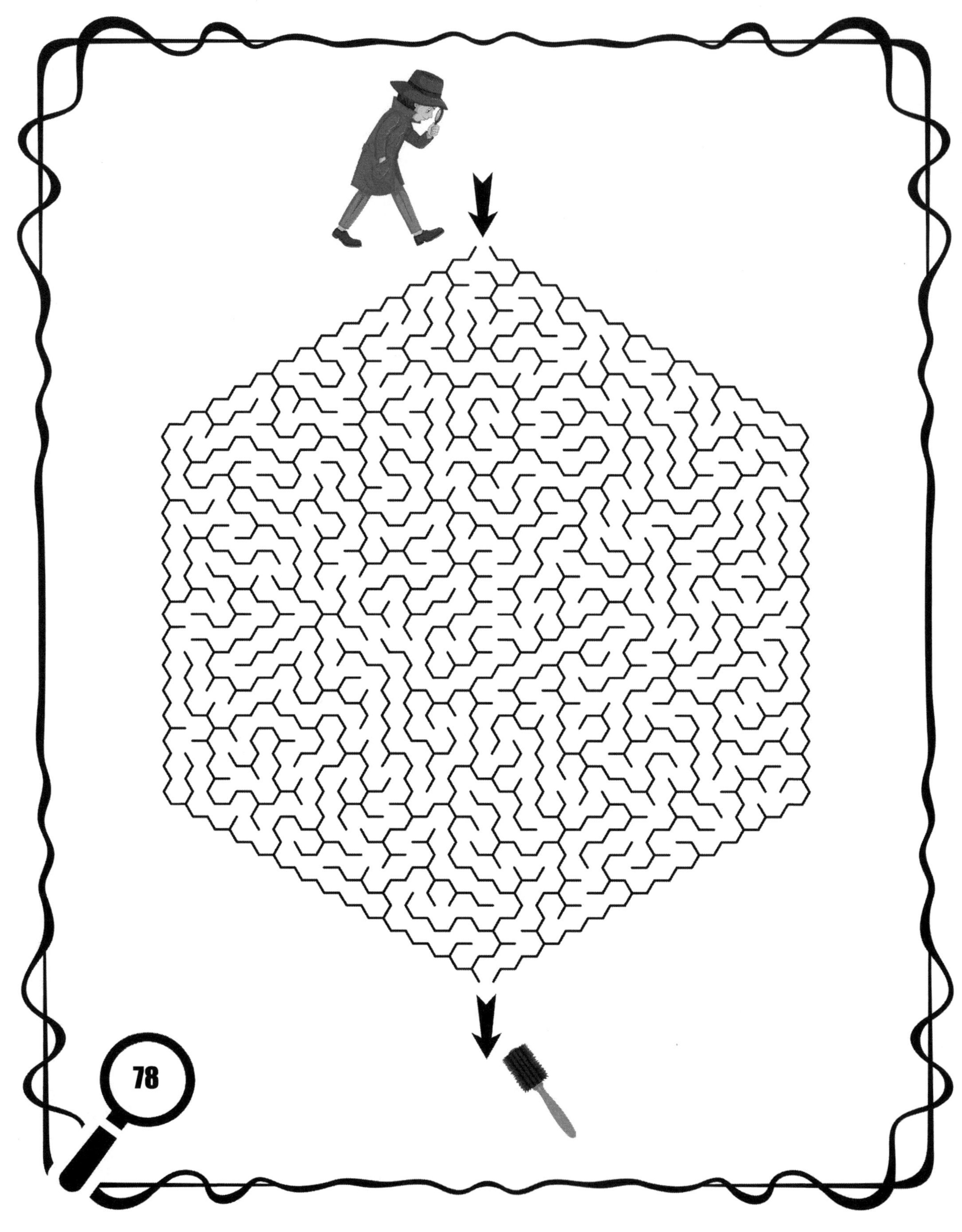

78

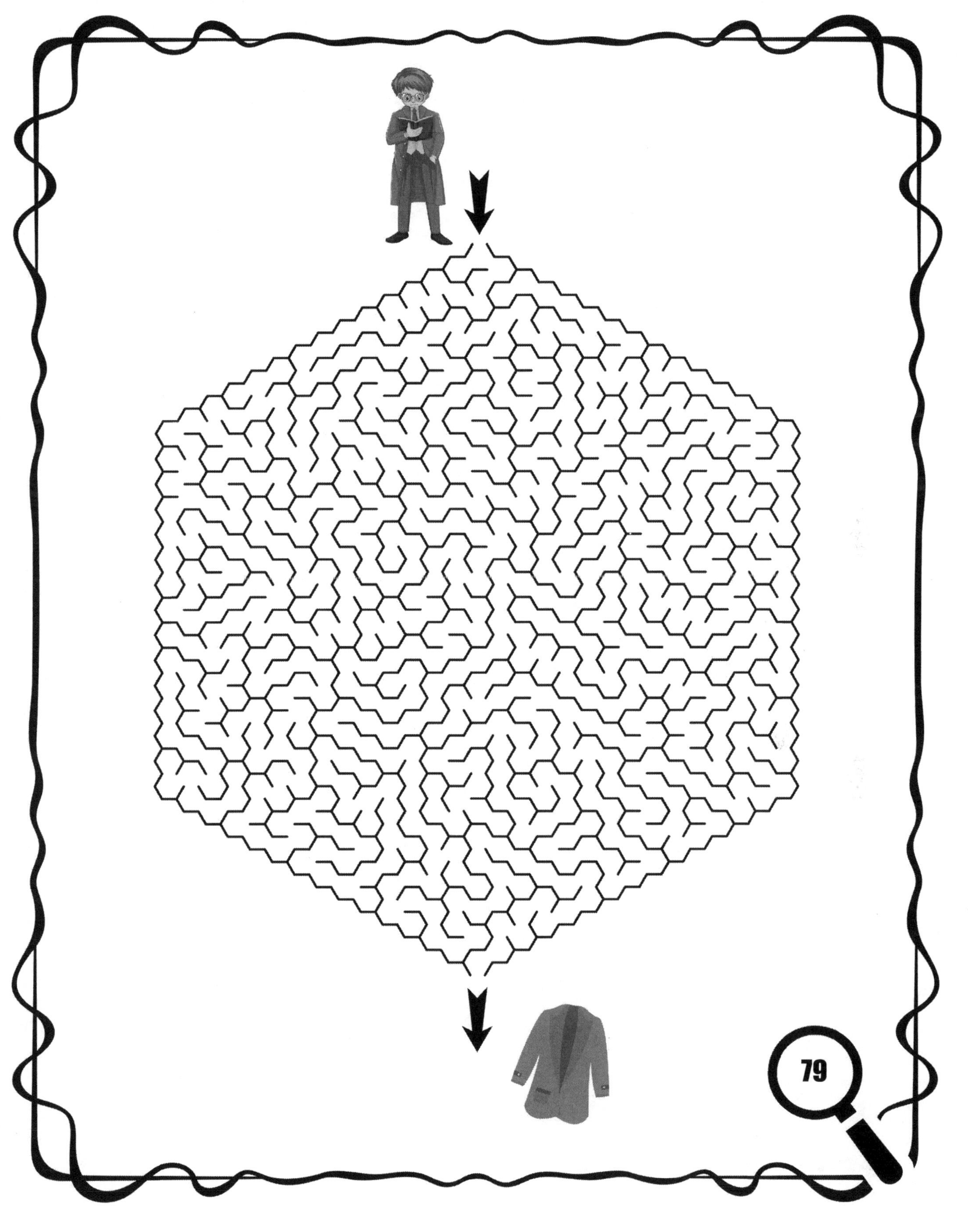

79

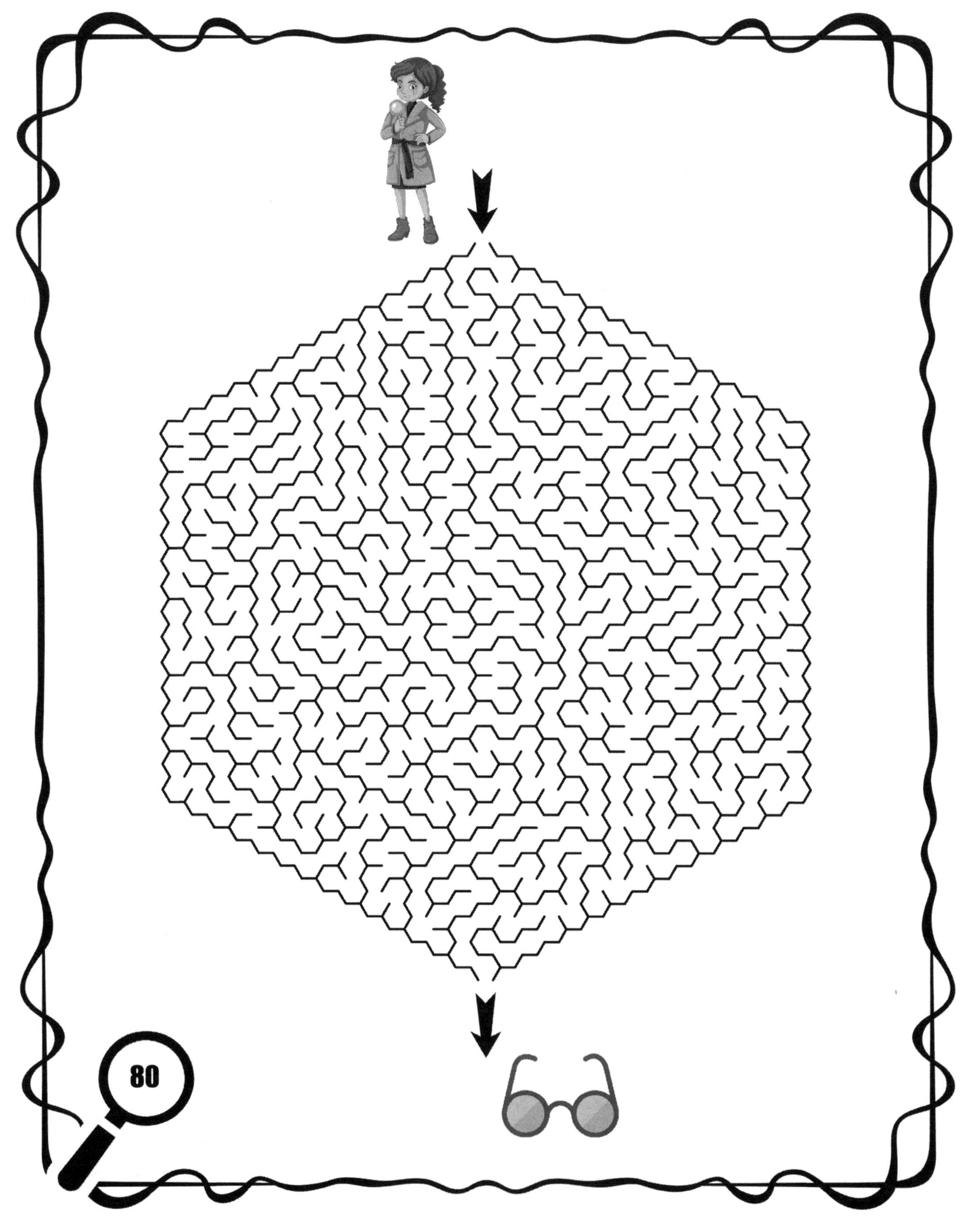
80

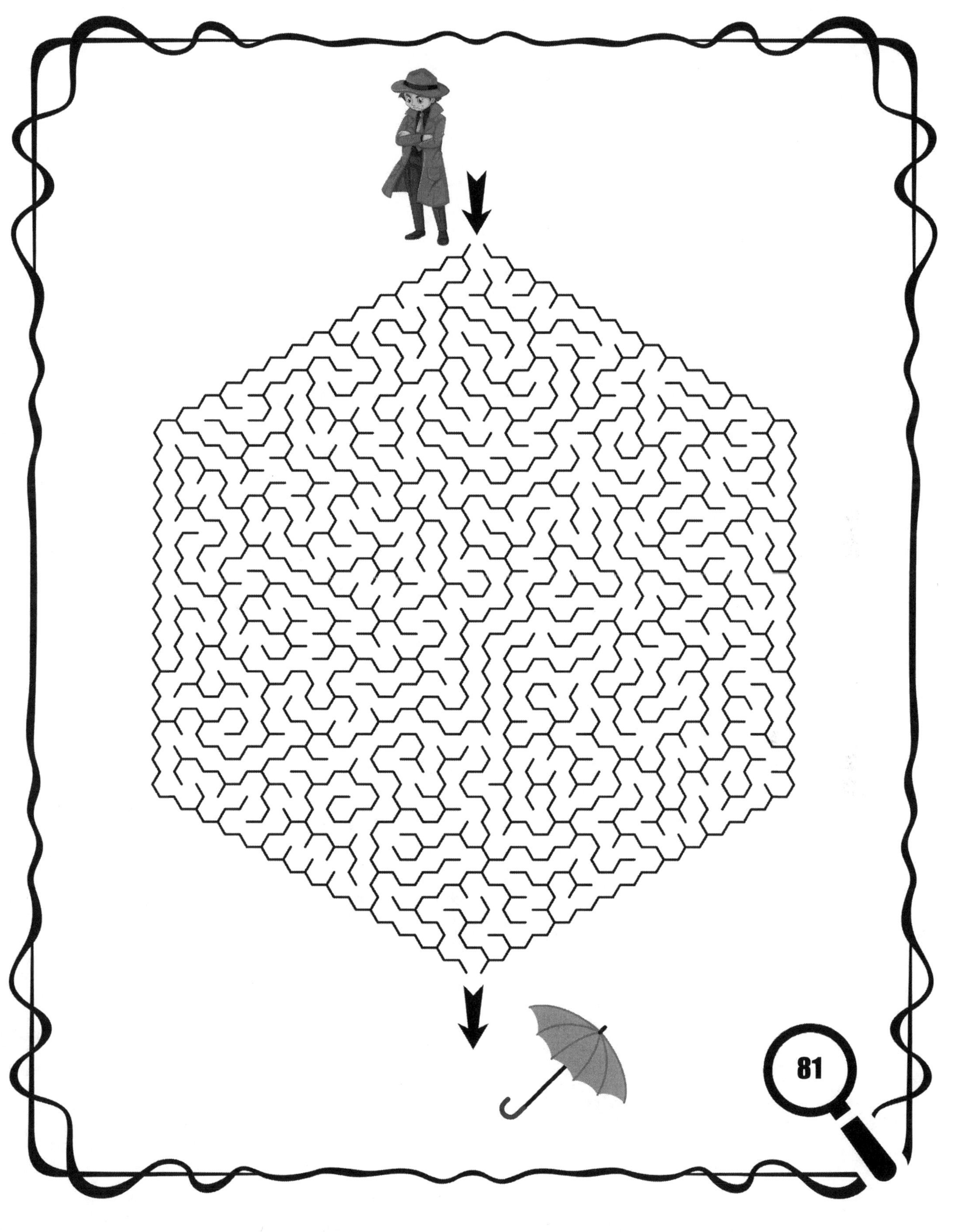

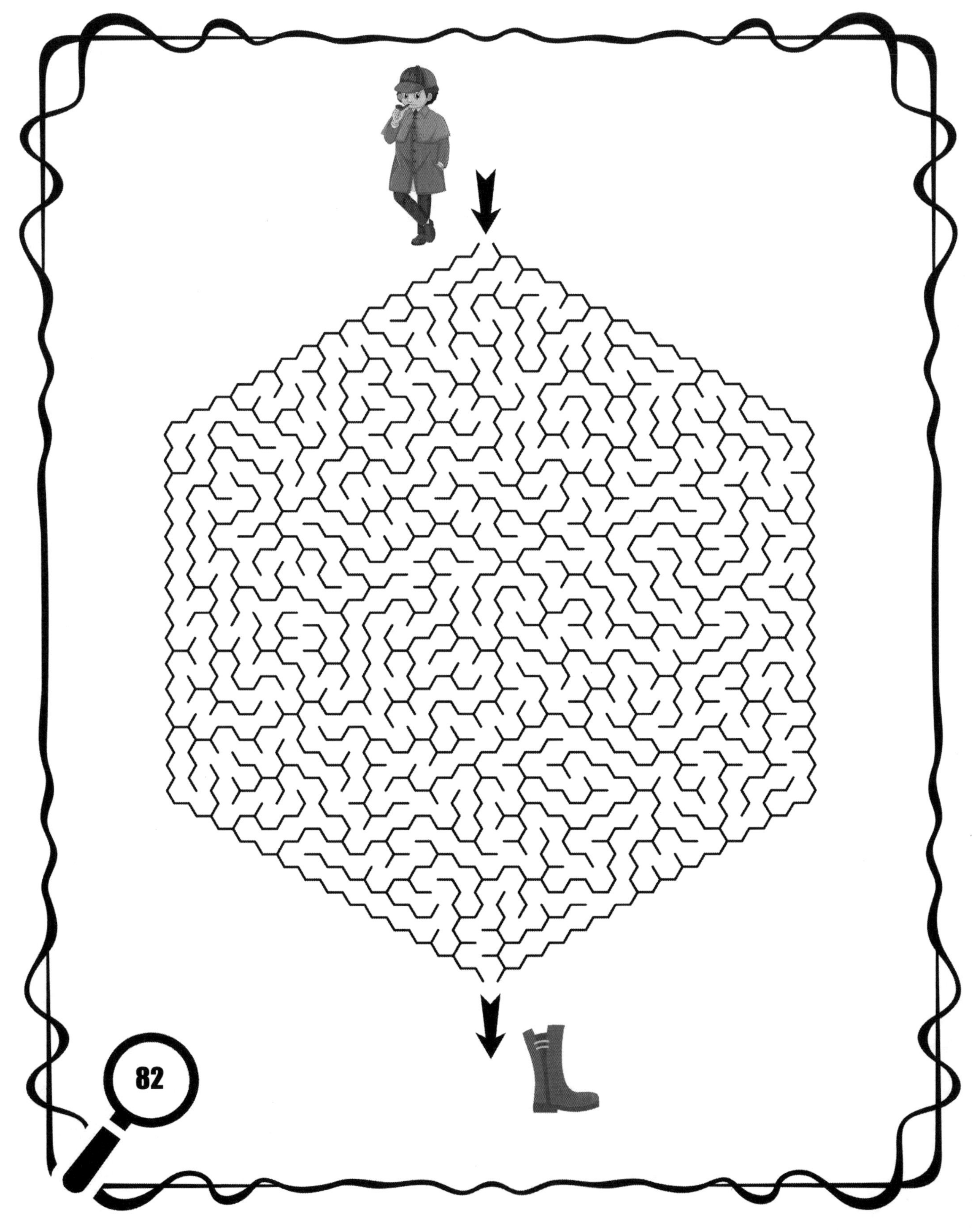

82

1

2

3

4

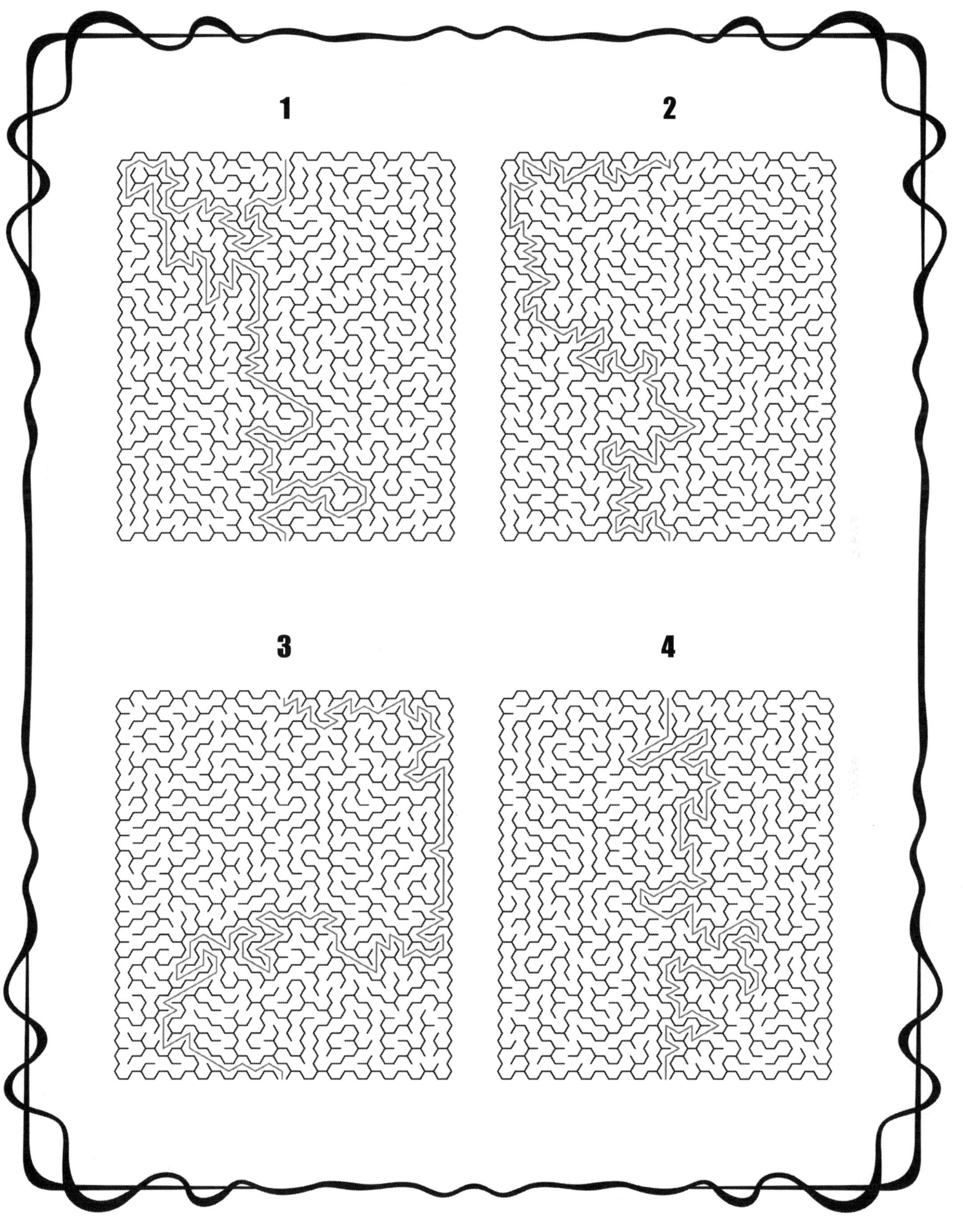

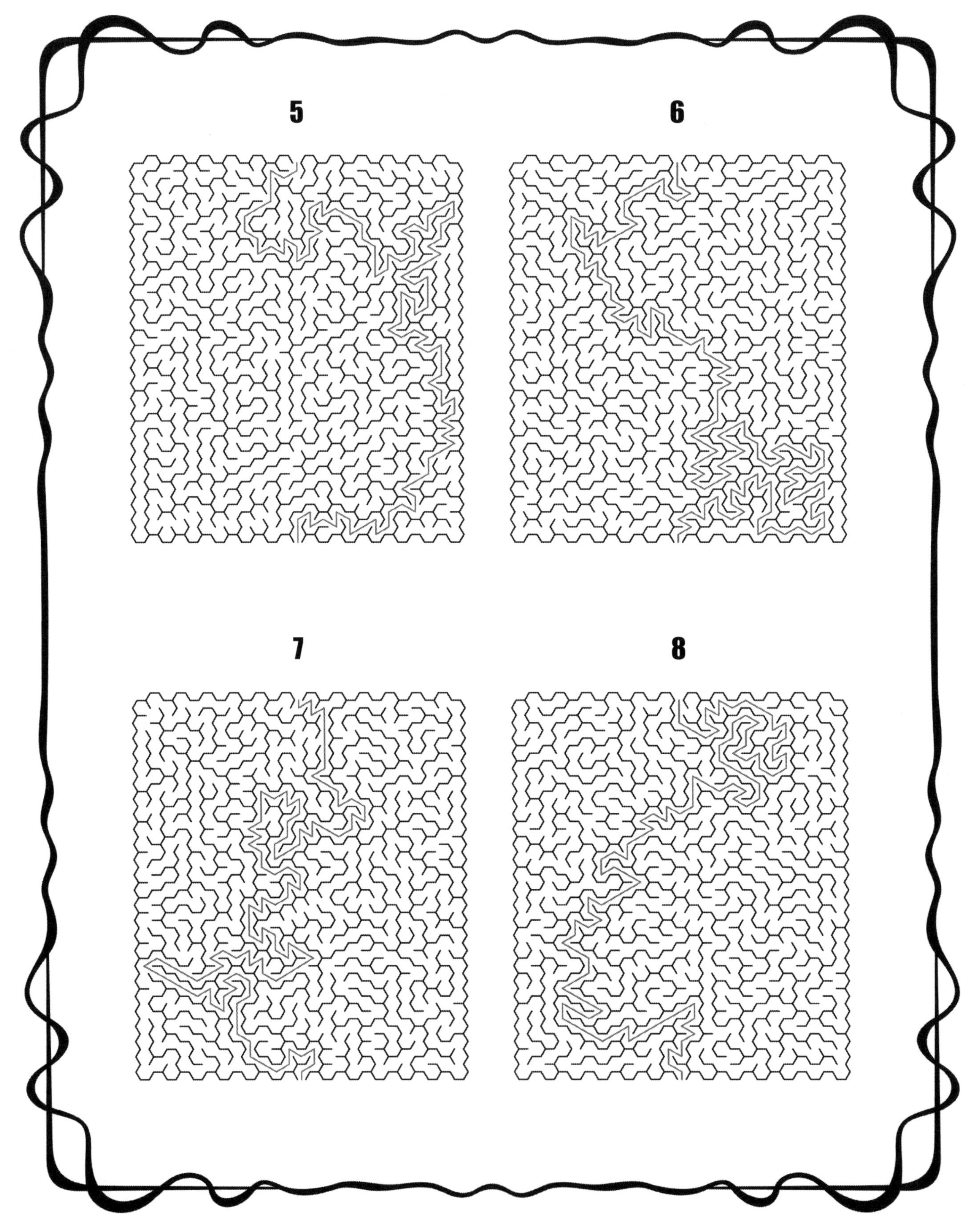
5
6
7
8

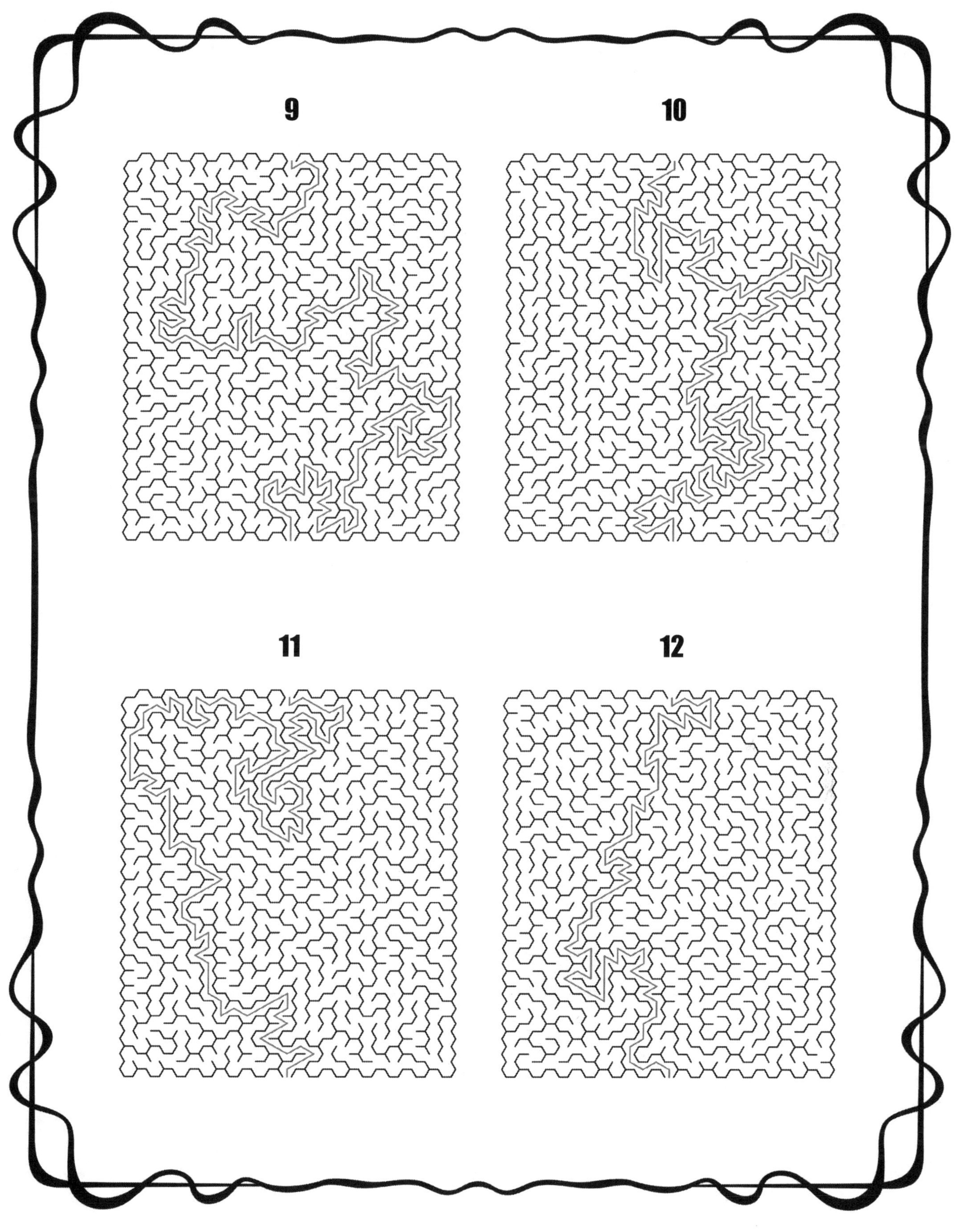
9
10
11
12

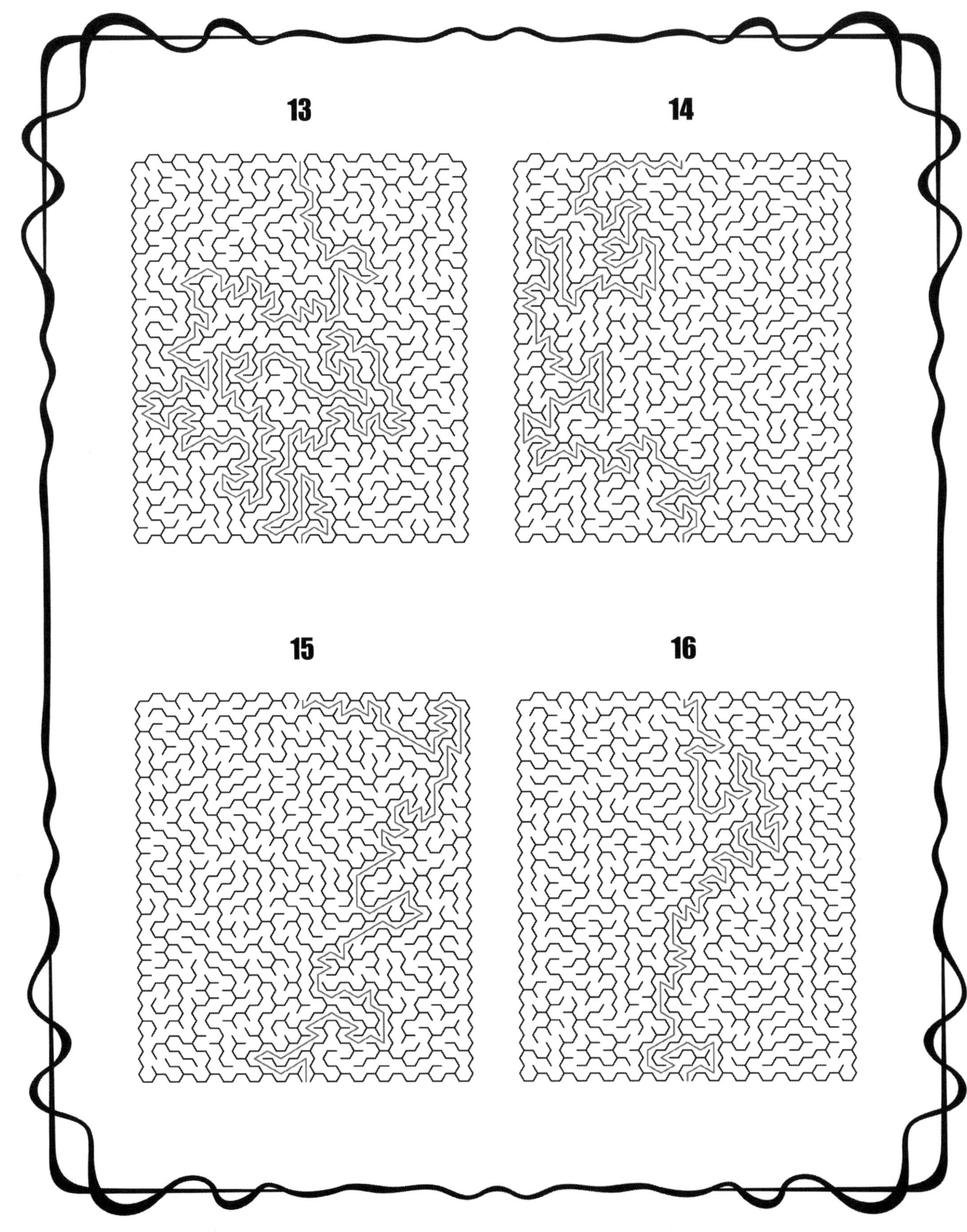

13
14
15
16

17

18

19

20

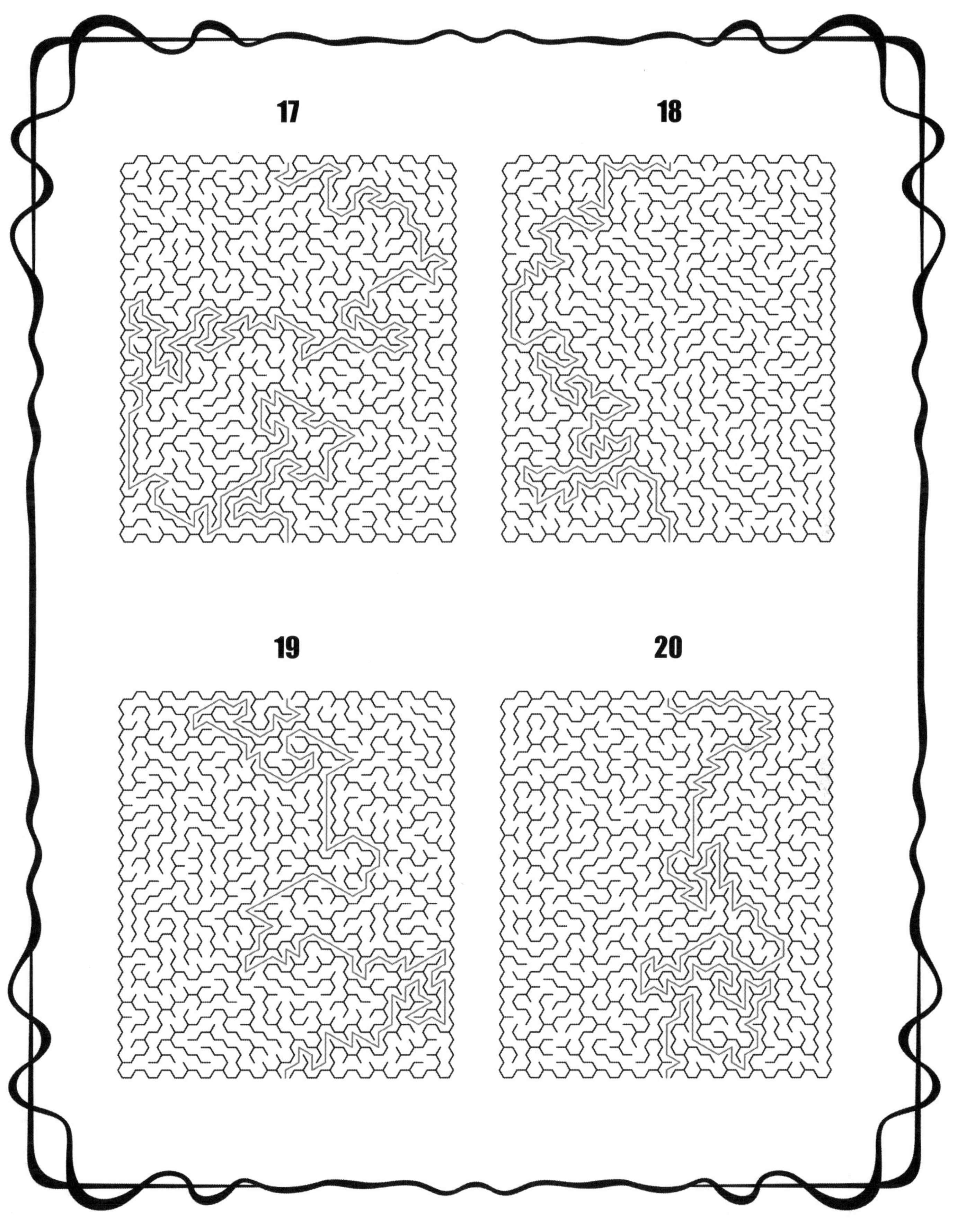

21

22

23

24

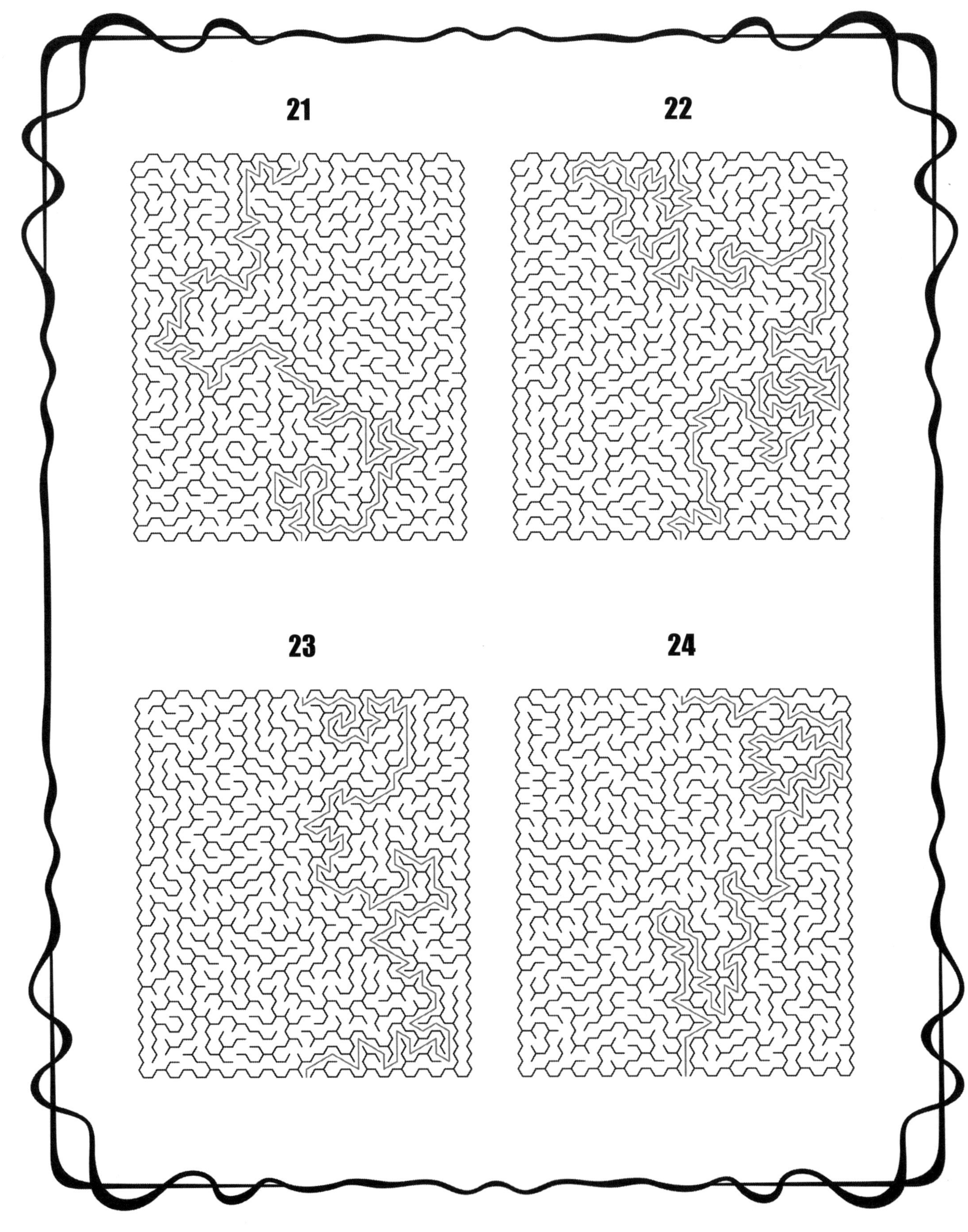

25

26

27

28

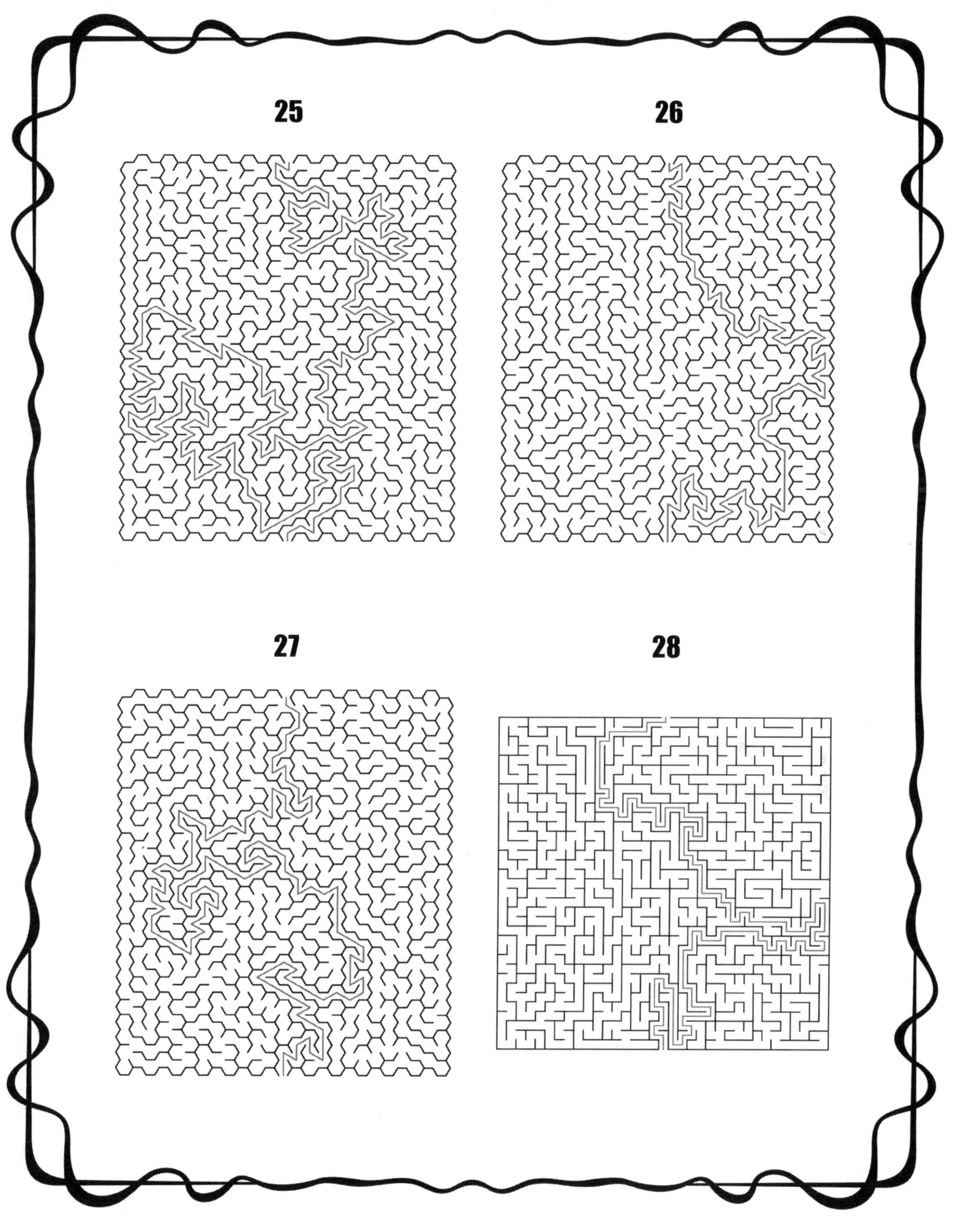

29

30

31

32

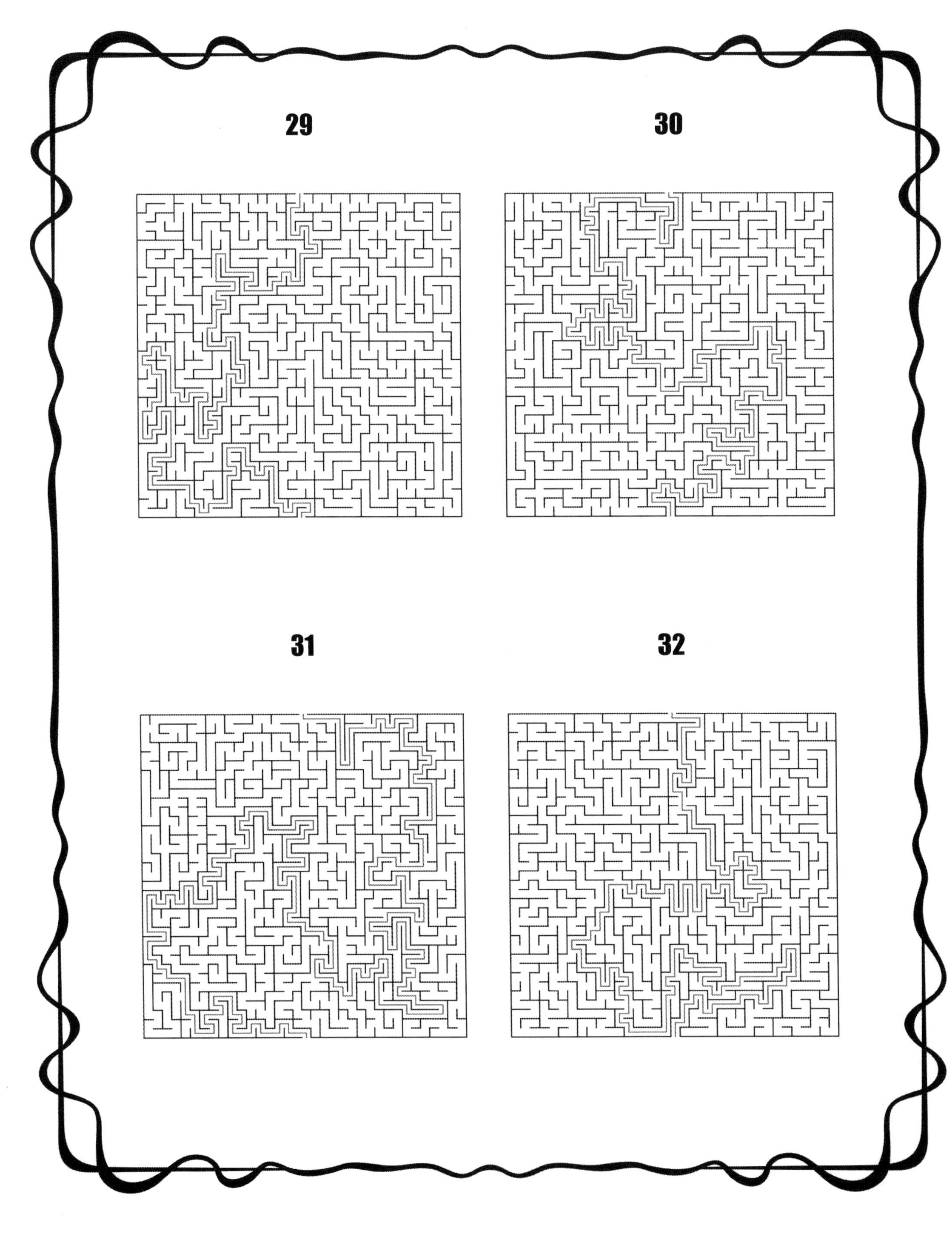

33

34

35

36

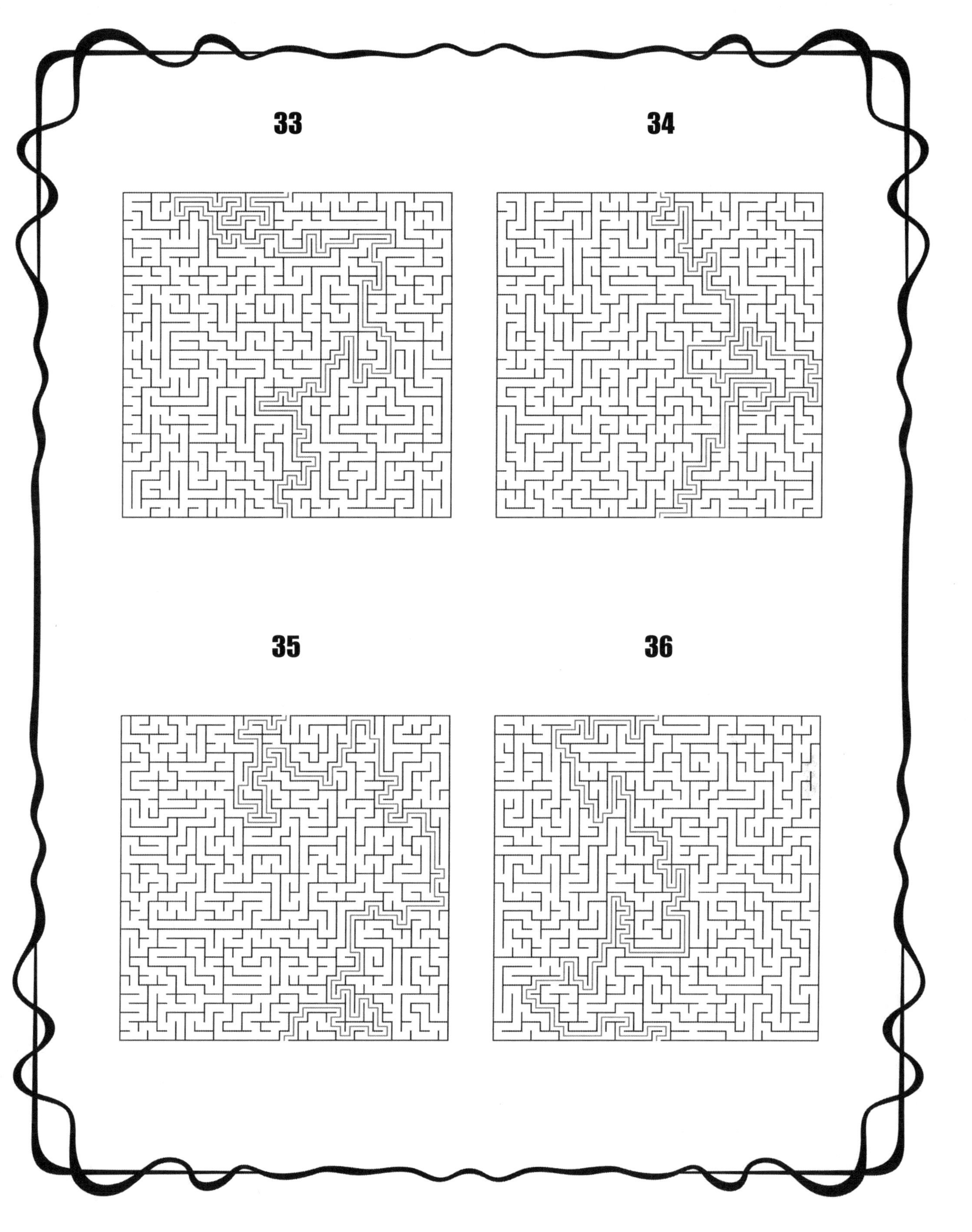

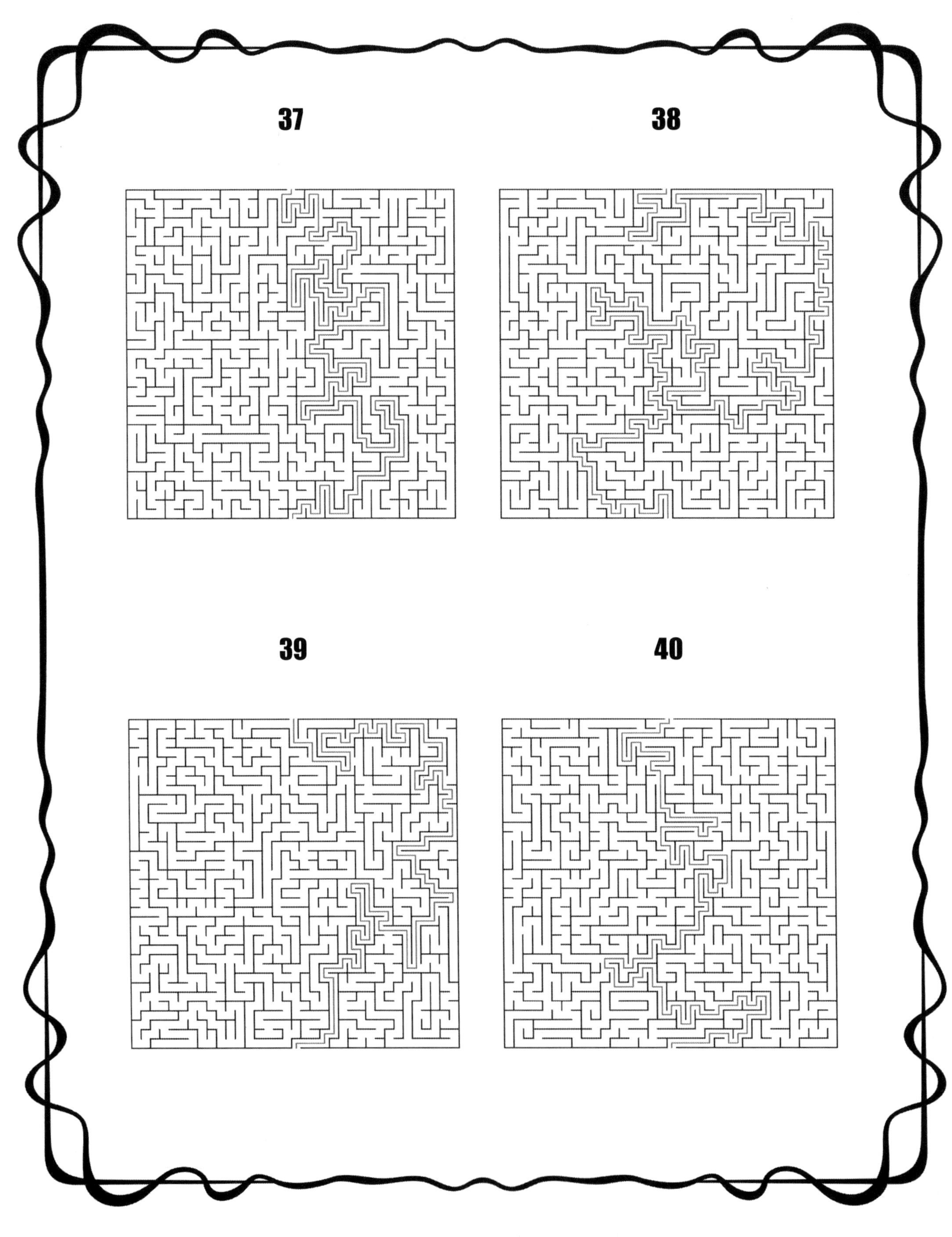
37
38
39
40

41

42

43

44

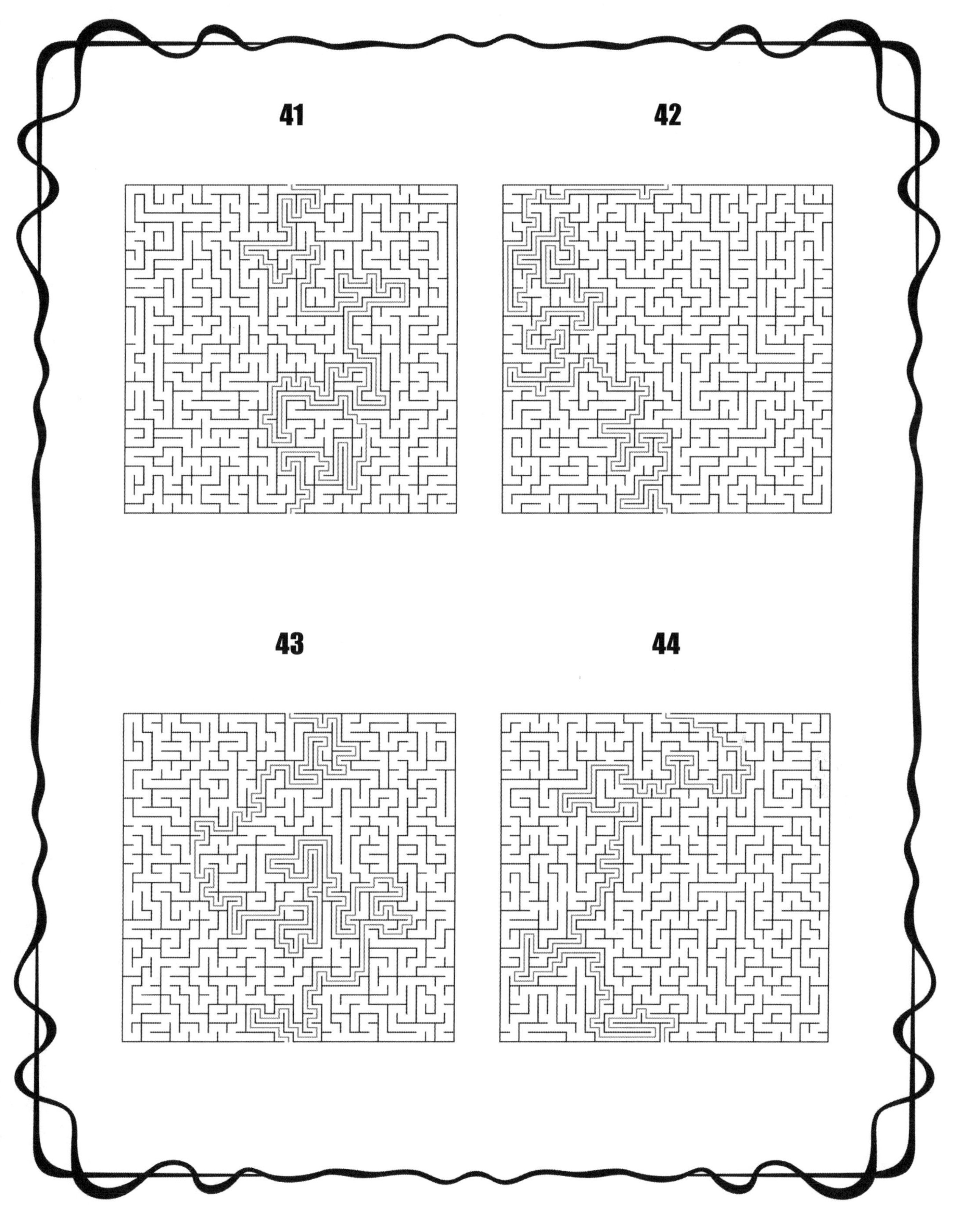

45

46

47

48

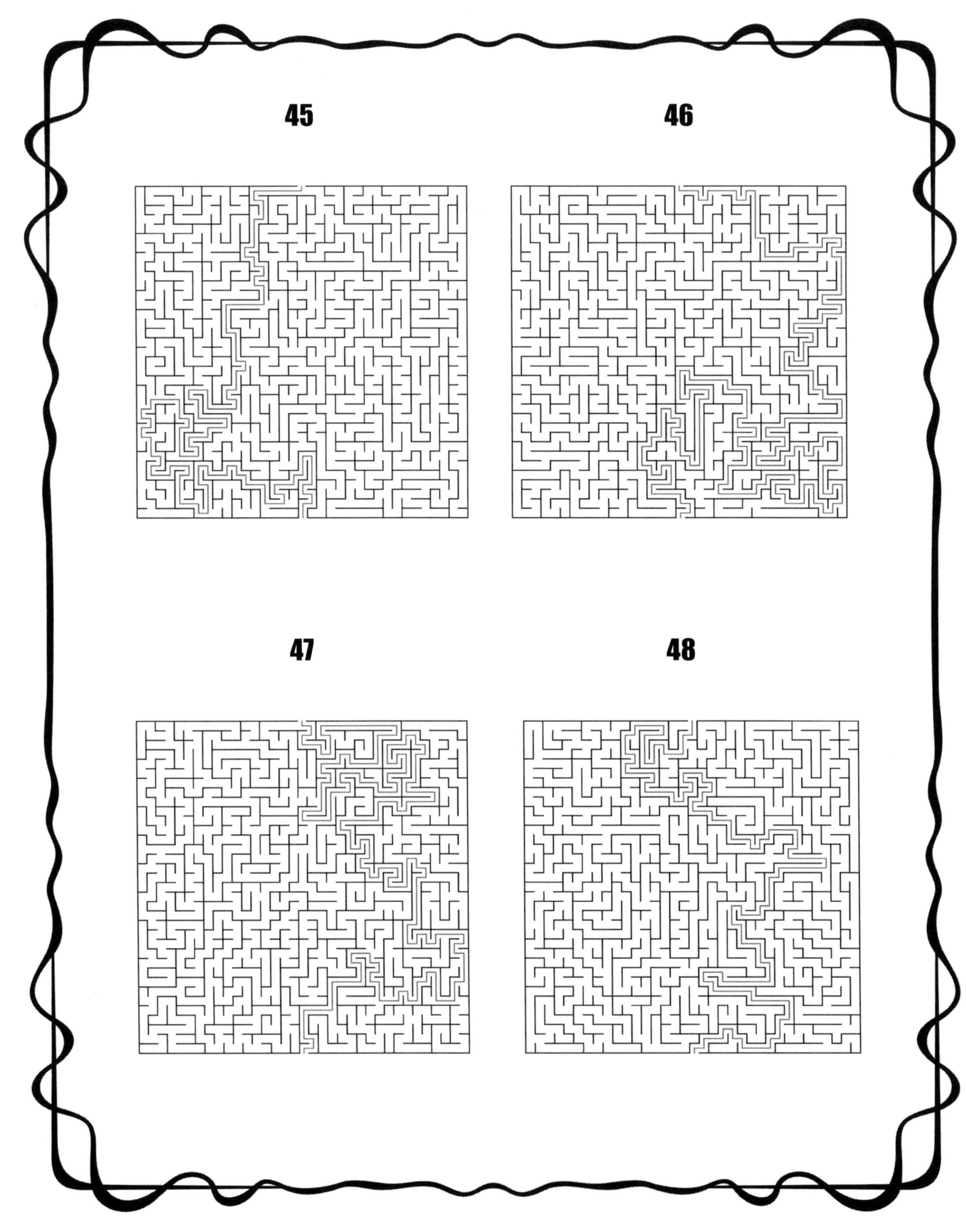

49

50

51

52

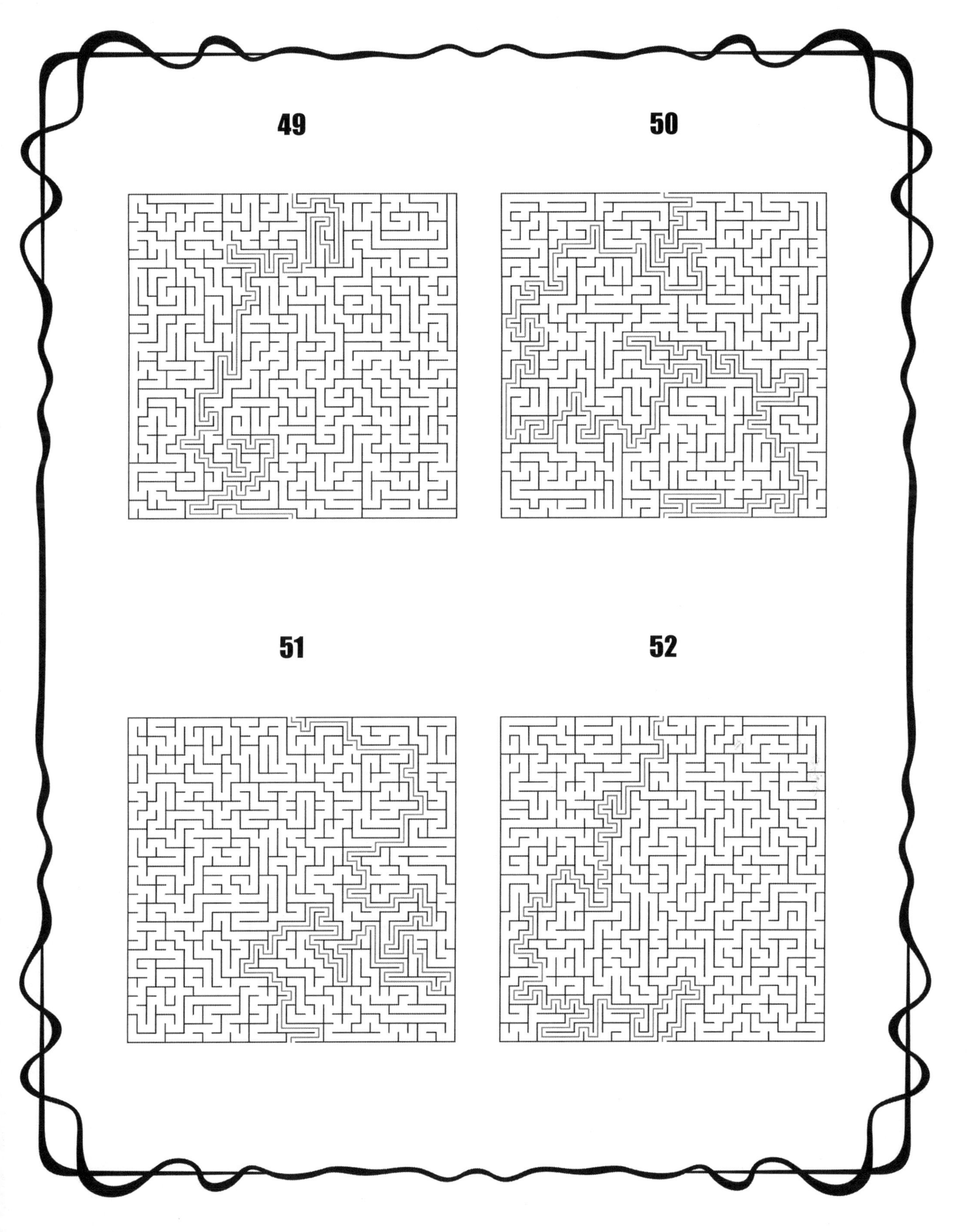

53

54

55

56

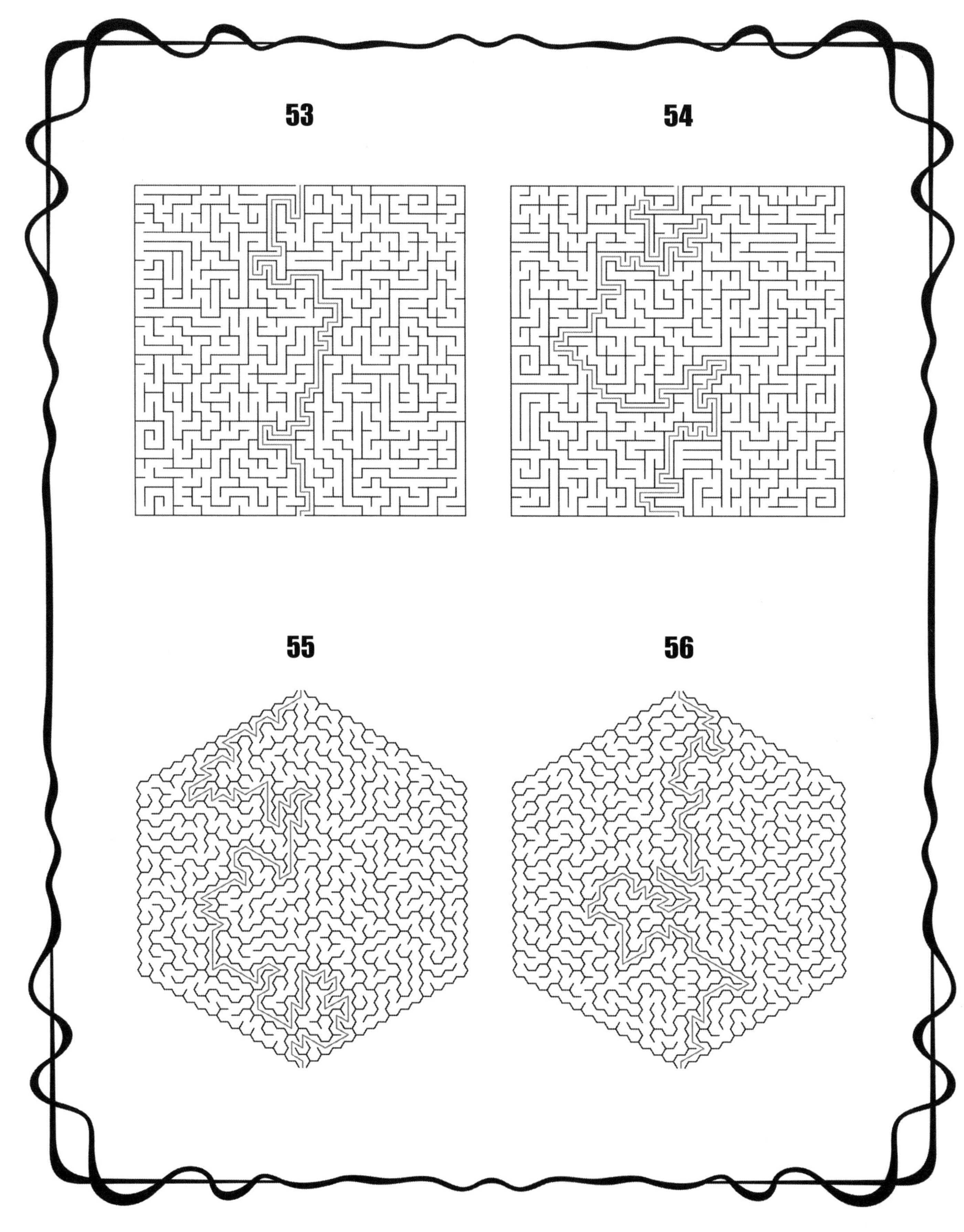

57

58

59

60

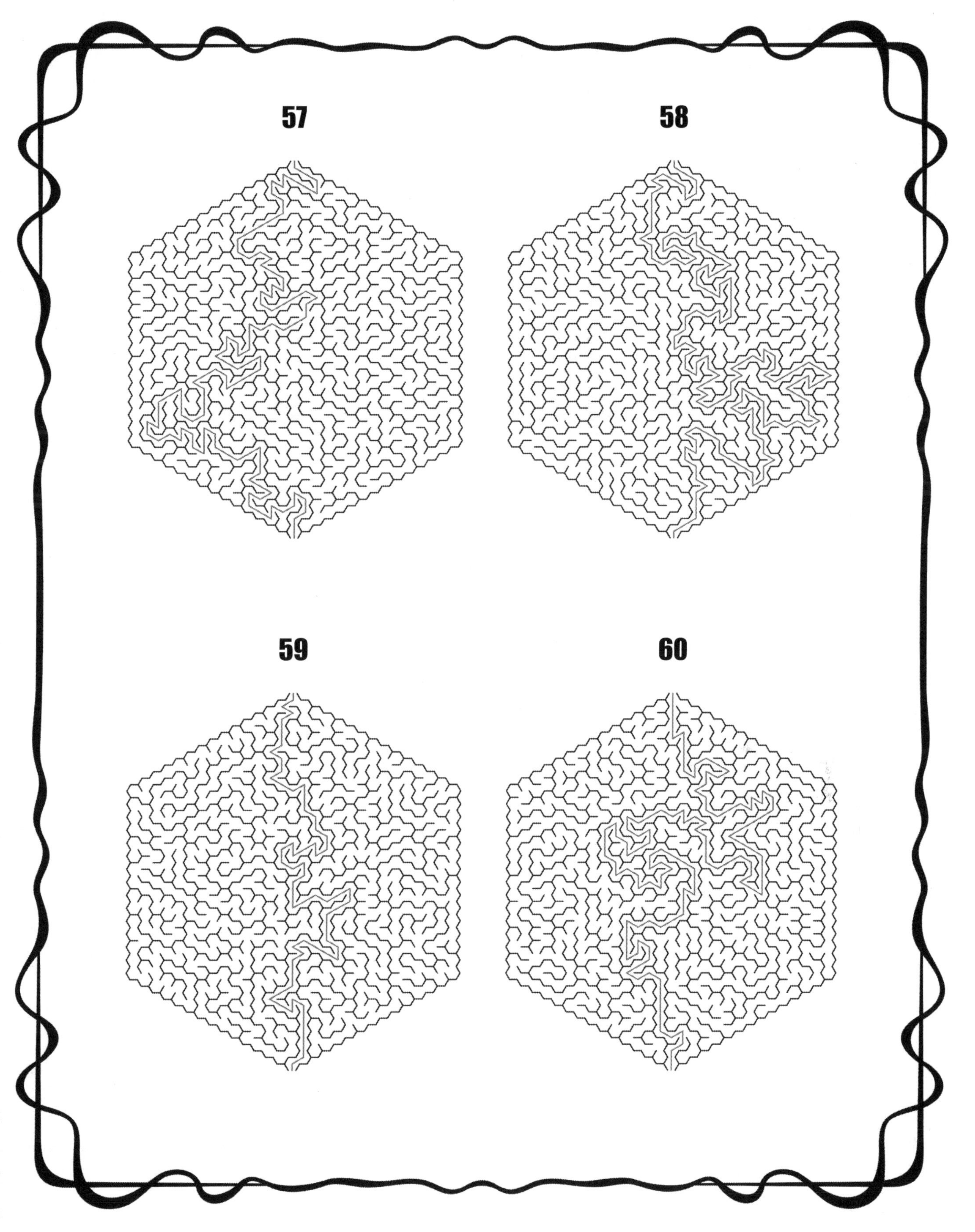

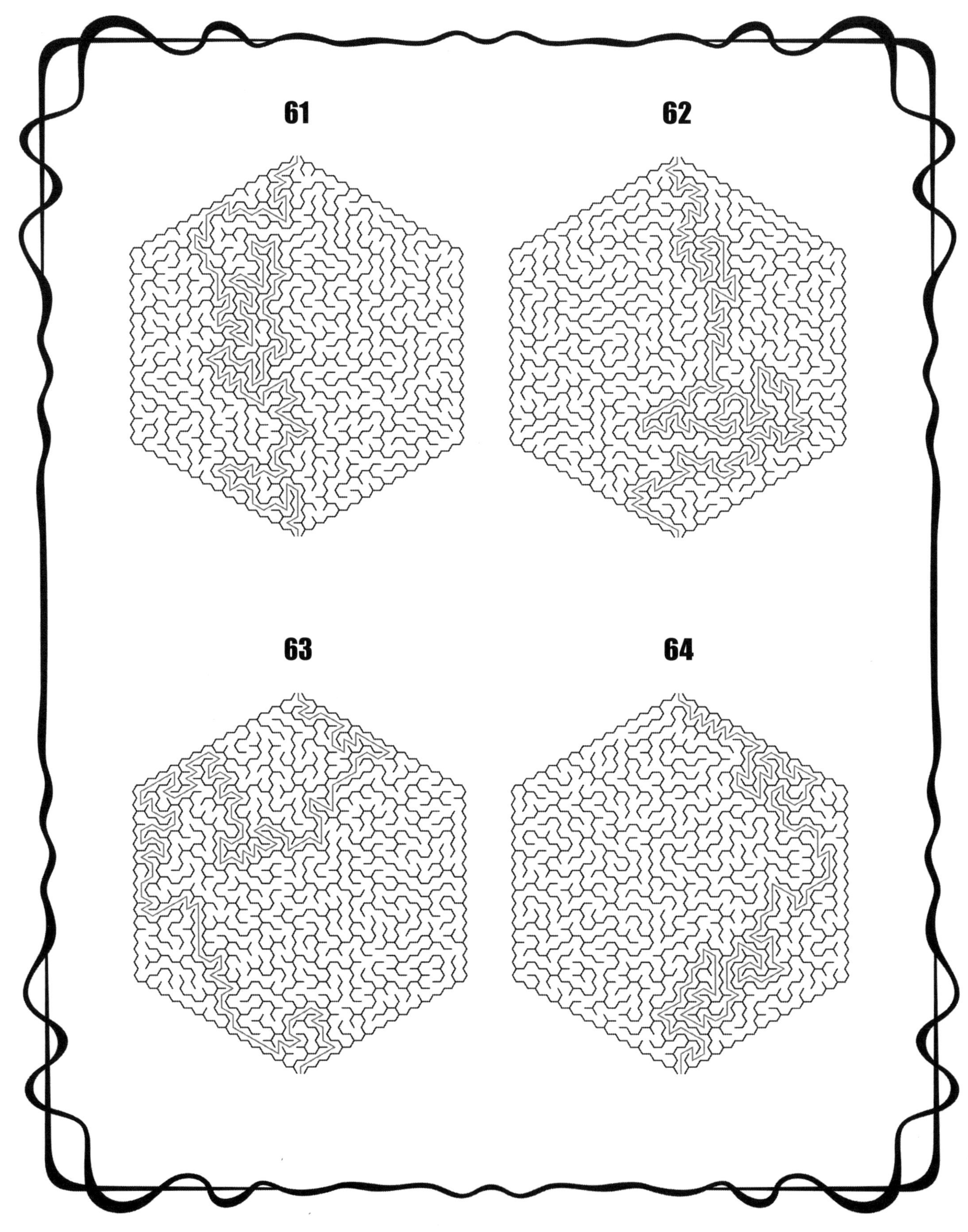

61
62
63
64

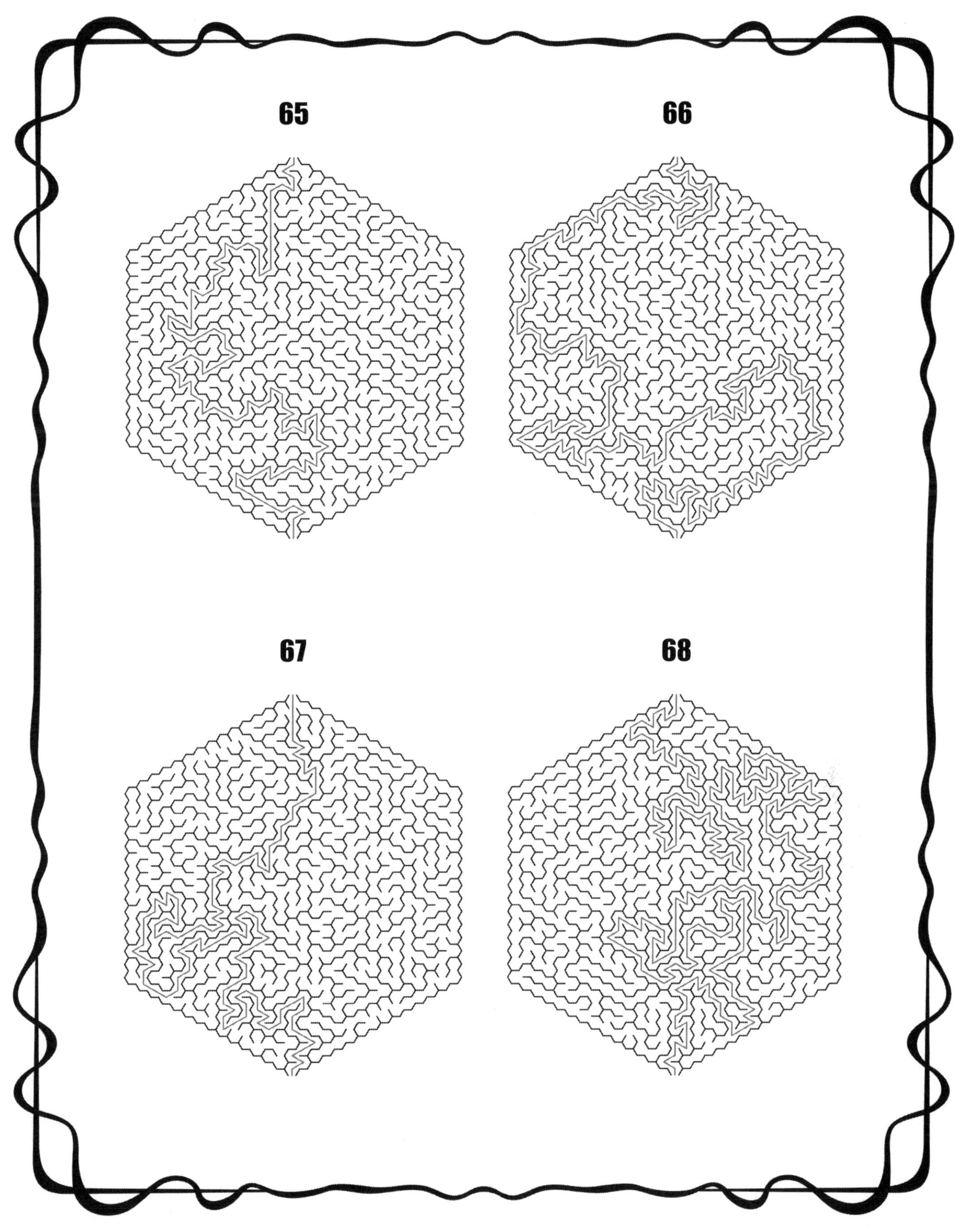
65
66
67
68

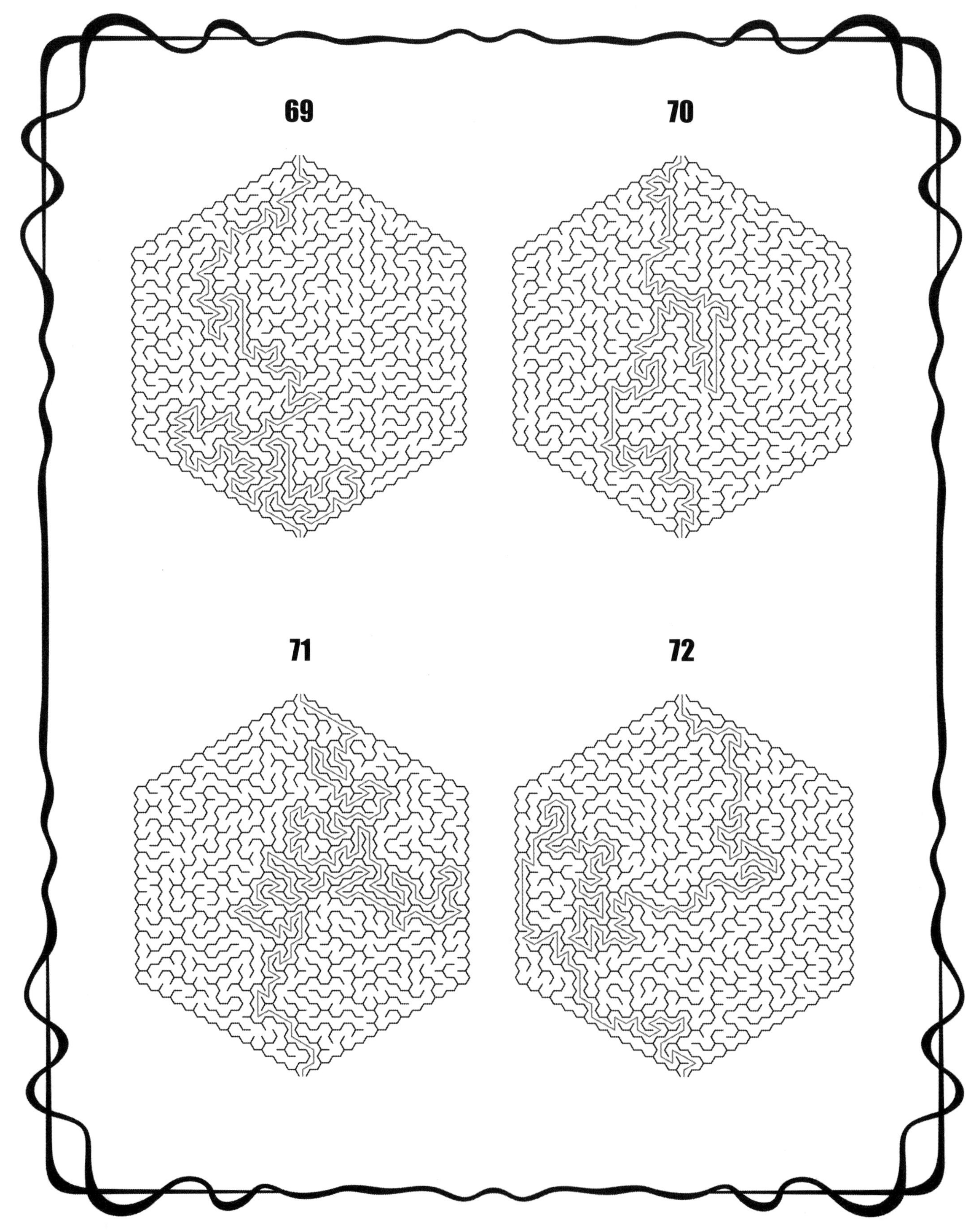

69
70
71
72

73

74

75

76

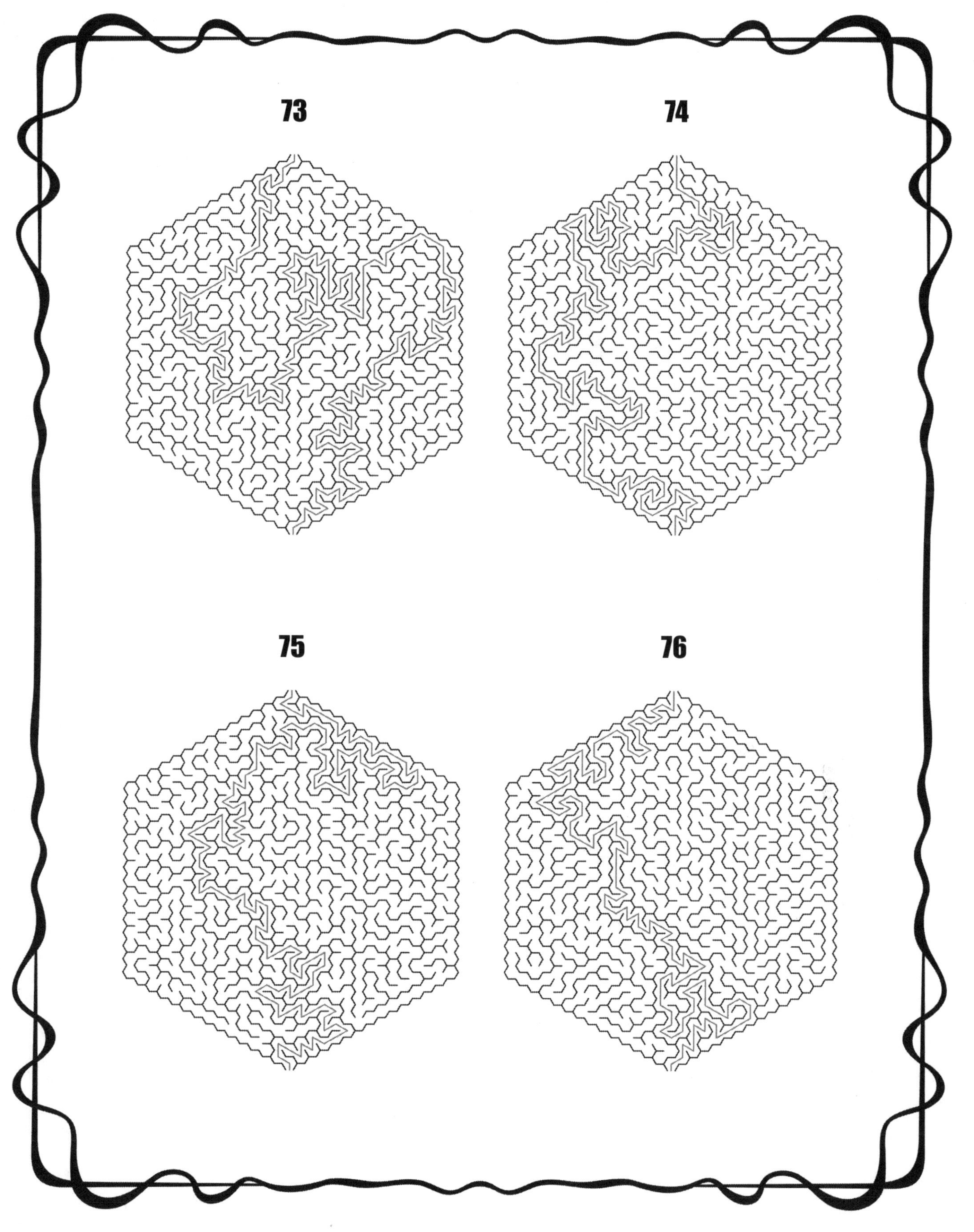

77

78

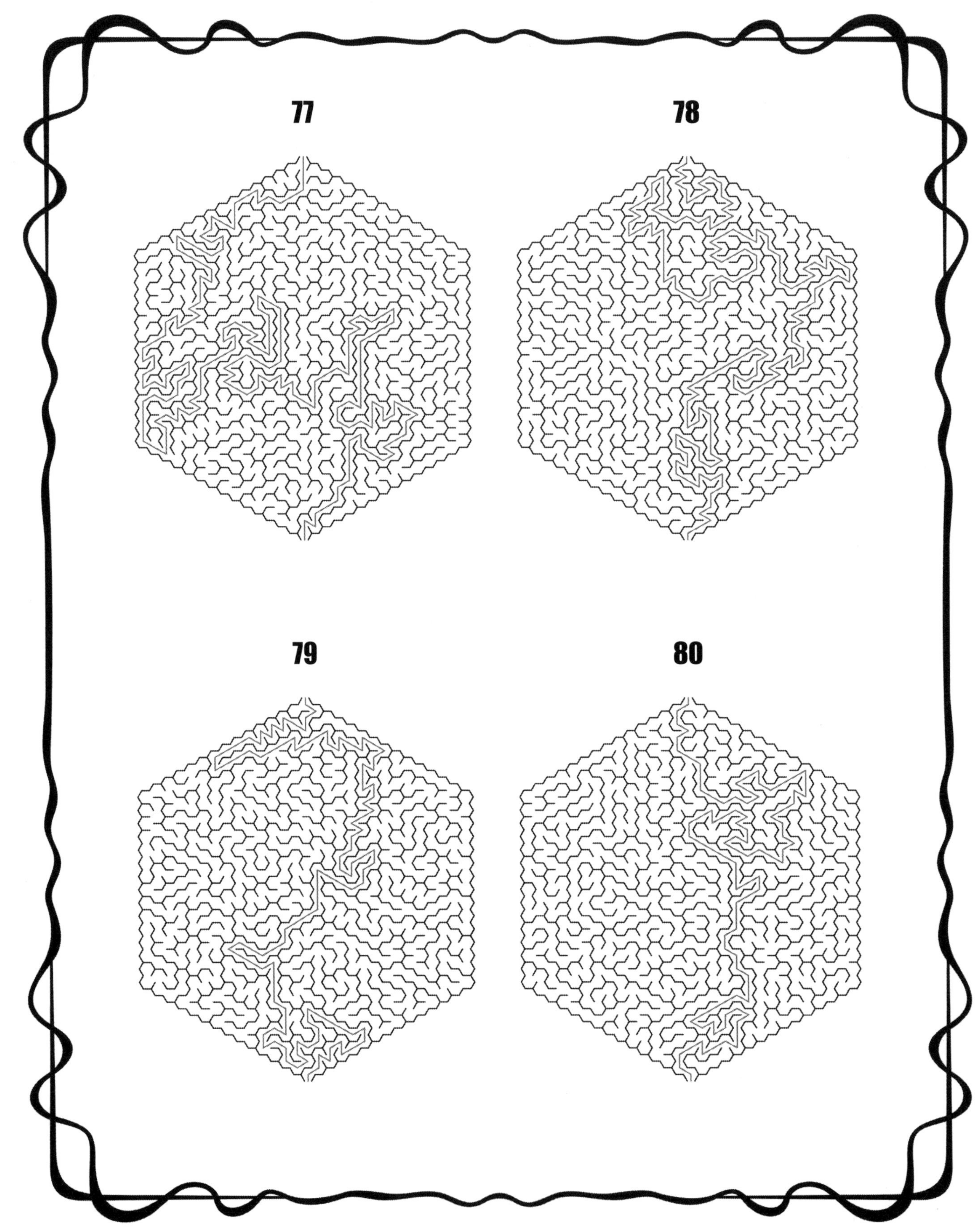

79

80

81

82

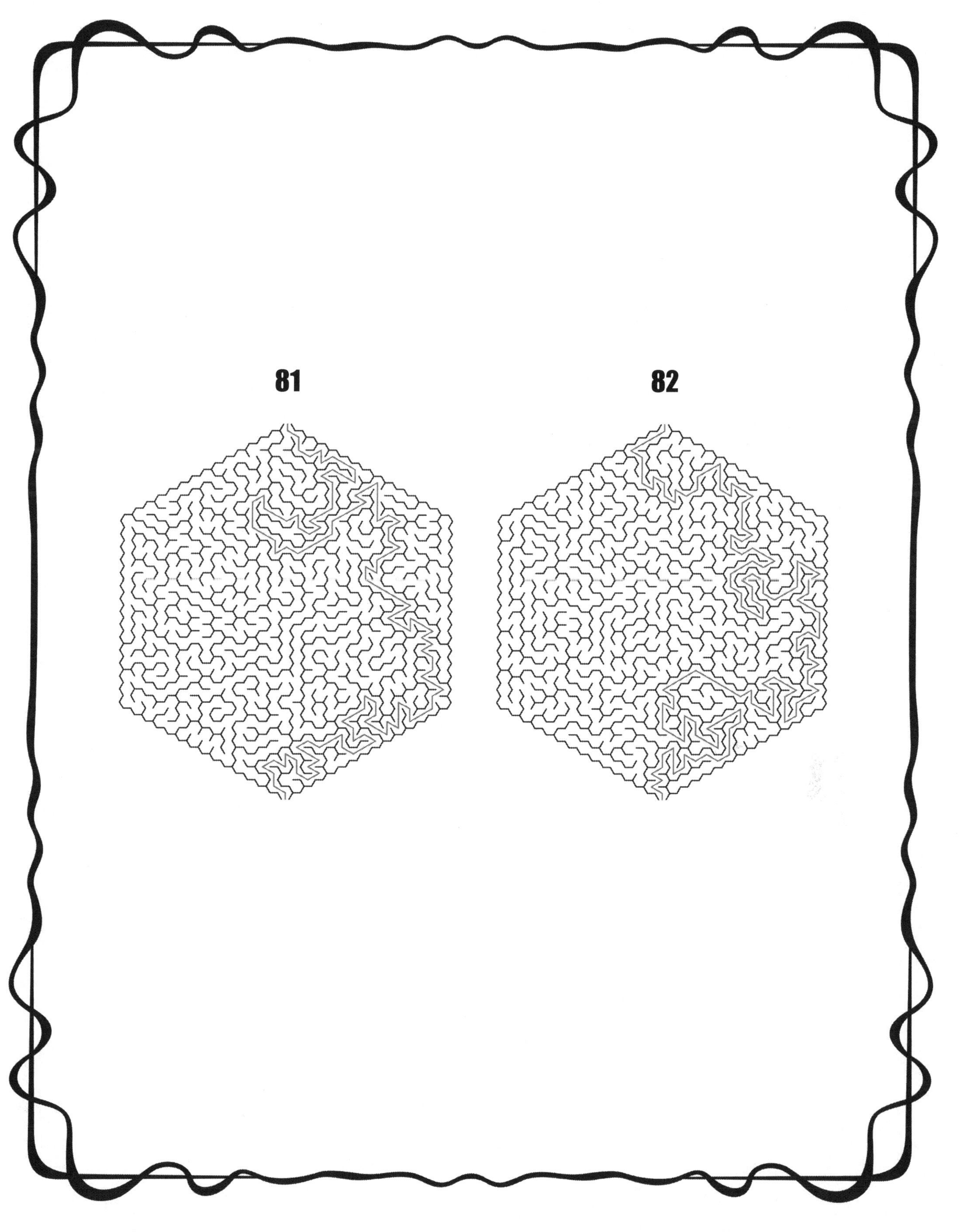